Going to Meet George

Going to Meet George

AND OTHER OUTINGS

Ronald Blythe

Ronald Blythe

LONG BARN BOOKS

For Ian and Joachim

PUBLISHED BY
LONG BARN BOOKS

Ebrington, Gloucestershire GL55 6NW

First published in 1999
1 3 5 7 9 10 8 6 4 2

Copyright © Ronald Blythe, 1999

Set in 11/14pt Monotype Columbus
Printed by Redwood Books, Trowbridge

ISBN 1 902 4210 3 5

Contents

The Artist Plantsman

I have usurped this title from the little book which John Nash wrote just before his death. He would sit by the fire and juggle his preferences for what he would be, given his time over again. Eventually he settled on the following order: musician, gardener, artist. No, no! we protested. Back to front. 'Well then, artist-plantsman and plenty of piano.' And so he was beguiled into putting down a few words about his art plus his passion which was for flowers. We give the dying something to do to pass the remaining time. John was not deceived. He would put on 'Chairman Mao', the padded cotton coat which Natalie had brought him from China, and, if the sun shone, 'Rommel' the desert cap with its neck-shield, and with difficulty make his way outside. And there he would look and look with no small despair, for the jungle was encroaching on that fertile East Anglian spot where one had only to show a cutting the soil for it to shoot. Gloom, gloom. 'The garden is going and I am going ...' No, no John! And I would set-to among his nettles. 'Mind your big feet among the lilies!' Yes, John. 'Girlie' gardeners arrived spasmodically to prune and propagate, and he would survey their upturned bottoms with frank pleasure. Also a large mower, whose efforts to start the Hayter were interspersed with grunts and curses. So there was help. Yet still the garden rioted. Christine, John's wife, had taken her last walk through it on her way to a dinner-party and then, incomprehensibly to him – for she had hidden her illness from him – had died. All over a weekend. 'What did she mean, going off like that?' He was astonished. They had been married for over half a century. She used to tell me about their discovering Bottengoms Farm during the war, how she was inside wondering if it could ever be made habitable, and John was outside shouting, 'Yes, yes, this is it!' For it was one of those places with at least six kinds of soil, from glorious earth to soggy marsh, and a sand patch thrown in. Also horse-ponds. 'I never pass up a good pond.' There were youthful snaps of me raking them out, dressed only in muddy Y-fronts.

'What will you do here all on your own when I'm gone?'

'Look after your garden, John.'

He looked sceptical. The final year wore on and in that September he went. But the garden showed no sign of going, allowing for its annual capacity for huge weeds. There remains still at this late twentieth century hour many a garden which continues to breathe the principles of managed profusion advocated by William Robinson and his disciples, of whom John was one. The antecedents of such gardening were everywhere, in the bookshelves, in the tumbling granary, under stones even. Tucked away in the clefts of neglected trees. Simply look, and there they were. The Nashes were inclined to put things away, rather than throw things away. So they mouldered but existed. It made for good archaeology. So I read for the first time Robinson's influential masterpiece *The English Flower Garden* (1883) and the old catalogues from Six Hills Nursery, sent to John by his earliest gardener friend Clarence Elliott, and then John's own last garden will and testament, *The Artist Plantsman*, after which Bottengoms Farm 'came together' as one might say.

As a boy in still rural Iver before World War One, John had observed how a group of elderly sisters who lived down the road virtually ignored the formal grounds which surrounded their house and went on gardening what had once been their childhood patches, cramming them with 'treasures' which they had begged, stolen or borrowed from wherever they happened to 'discover' them. His eyes were opened and he saw that what his father called 'the garden' was in fact a croquet lawn edged with dull beds. I too then recalled that my first true garden had belonged to aged neighbours, a mother and daughter, a place dense with what they described as their ' bits', and which made a ravishing cushion of flowers and scents threaded with winding dirt paths just wide enough for them to shuffle along to pat and encourage. They pronounced flowers 'flors', which I was told was 'Norfolk.'

It was Clarence Elliott who took John Nash into the horticultural scene proper during the Twenties. 'I used to draw the plants he had collected on his expeditions to the Andes and the Falkland Islands and elsewhere, not excluding finds in English gardens, which he maintained were the best hunting-ground.' And it was John and another old friend, Stephen Garrett the Cambridge botanist, who introduced me to the world of the plant-hunter. Not that I was ever able to do much more than listen and look. All the same, it was a green education which I now realized stretched back decades before I was born and, as writers tend to do, I became intrigued by having such direct links with a gardening past. I noticed the Empire's contribution, and the pre-tourism Mediterranean contribution. Two more of John's friends, and eventually mine, were Jock Cranbrook who, in 1932, had accompanied Frank Kingdon Ward on planthunting journeys in the Far East, and Cedric Morris who, every winter would desert Suffolk for Portugal or Morocco, returning like a swallow in April, though weighted down with unusual luggage, precious seeds and plants buried in his canvasses.

But then the least travelled gardeners of their generation expected to keep pace with the plant-hunters. Garden imports and exports brought natives and exotics together all over the globe. Raj exiles took Mrs Earle's *Pot-Pourri from a Surrey Garden* (1897) to Simla, and A.E.P. Grierson *The Evolution of the Mogul Gardens of the Plains of India.* did some evolving itself in the Home Counties. It was Grierson who made a floral background for the 1912 Durbar and Miss Jekyll, of course, who planted the beds of Vice-Regal Lodge, Delhi. And it was much due to English gardeners born in India, like Eleanour Sinclair Rohde, for example, that a certain sensuousness invaded the gardening scene back home. Her *The Scented Garden, The Old World Pleasaunce* and *Gardens of Delight* introduced a languorous element which was quite disturbingly opposite to that created by carpet-bedding and ball-games. Nice, fat, battered old gardening books such as these lie around in the house, each one a treat. Their inter-war equivalent were Marion Cran's *The Garden of Experience* and *Garden of Good Hope.* John liked Dean Hole. S. Reynolds Hole, Dean of Rochester, patron saint of roses and cyclists, looked like Gregory Peck. He launched devastating attacks on the lawns-and-bedding-out gardeners who had destroyed the rich muddled gardens of his youth, with their mystery and glorious tangles.

Bottengoms would have delighted the Dean. Seeing some of the tools there, a visitor asked if I collected old implements. As these were in everyday use, I was briefly puzzled. I then realised how very ancient they were, not least things like the roller, the mighty ladders and the right-angled fork for dragging the ditch. The most evocative utility was a little greenhouse which had belonged to Eric Ravilious and given to John by his widow after the war. It appears in Ravilious's woodcuts and it may have been one of those Duncan Tucker glasshouses which cost £14.10s in the Thirties. By the time I inherited it it had rotted, bowed, swayed. I saved its glass. It had long been empty of plants save convolvulus and marestail, but there was plenty of horticultural social history on its cracking shelves – a Rippingille heater, lumps of crazy paving, tins of Katakiller, Eureka and Corry's White Fly Death, and lots of pale seed-packets from long-ago springtimes. Ryder's seeds from St. Alban's, Dobbie's seeds from Edinburgh, Allwood's seeds from Hayward's Heath and John's favourite Thompson and Morgan's seeds from Ipswich. He had spent hours in Eric's old green-house, smoking like a trooper. Unlike now, one was seldom alone in the garden. There was always Len or some other man pottering about, often unseen yet companionable all the same. Both John Nash and Cedric Morris saw a good deal of 'girl' gardeners. They included John's sister Barbara, who ran a nursery near Princes Risborough and Beth Chatto, who was Cedric's brilliant pupil and whose garden at Elmstead contains some of his magic. Cedric would show us round his garden at Benton End with wild impropriety, laughing himself to tears at his own lewd botany, though every now and then changing his tack and becoming fascinatingly serious. Especially at iris-time. Some years after their deaths I sat outside at Bottengoms, and wrote some seasonal words.

SPRING

One can only be selective. As the sap rises, the ink flows; the writer penned-in all winter feels as let out in the first warm days as the cows from their sheds. What he sees has been seen countless times and countlessly recorded. But never mind. Spring gardens can bear repetition. Neither does the garden reader care as the familiar joyous clichés shoot across the page. 'Spring has returned,' wrote Rilke, 'and the earth is like a child that knows poems.' During spring I return now and then to two, never more contrasting women whose garden comment pleases me, Colette and Alison Uttley. I ask them to step forward from the multitude of authors who dig and tell, not because they are the best, but because each in her way is passionate – the only word – about the first flowers of the year, about spring air, spring everything. Their gardens are those of childhood, Castle Top Farm, Derbyshire: Manor Farm, Saint-Sauveur-en-Puissaye, Burgundy, gardens they carried with them everywhere for the rest of their lives. Alison Uttley's garden is that of chilly early spring, Colette's of approaching summer heat – although she knows how to revel in a good unseasonal shock, such as snow on roses. For both women spring-cleaning in the shape of billowing linen and released livestock, snap and cry just beyond their stone walls. Such farm gardens are for intelligent mothers to rear clever daughters in. Colette's mother, the incomparable Sido, has one overriding command. It is Look! Alison Uttley, the farmer's daughter who will grow up to be a scientist, did not require such an injunction. Her rural essays are brilliant with minutiae accurately witnessed and perfectly retrieved, especially that which deals with the muddles and small treasures of old farmhouse gardens.

The spring gardener is at his most tolerant when it comes to what Alison Uttley calls 'wildings.' Findings are her theme then, finding the first coltsfoot, the first white violets, the first cowslips. In a week or two there will be thousands, but the *first!* 'These flowers, the wild flowers and the ordinary little garden blossoms, were part of our life … They were brave immortals who were always beautiful … We felt we were immortals with them.' She declares that few wildings were ever refused a home, the dandelion, *dens leonis*, lion's tooth because of its sharply serrated leaves. But I give space to a noble dandelion here and there, and even Ragwort, the sighting of which brings on hysteria to visitors. In vain I quote John Clare –

> *Ragwort, thou humble flower with tattered leaves*
> *I love to see thee come and litter gold.*

It took me a long time to tolerate a fine dandelion in a flower-bed as it made its space during spring and promising a great kingly head. During my boyhood in Suffolk its double function as a disgraceful diuretic and as a clock blinded me to its splendour, although I did have a feeling of rapine when we decapitated it for wine. Alison Uttley is indifferent to what is and is not a garden-flower, especially in springtime. In fact there isn't much gardening done in her books. Things just come up, are recognised and welcomed. Like her, they withstood the Derbyshire cold ('The word "December" was like music to me,') and all through February, March and April she would receive them back with a mixture of good botany and frank lyricism. However, it being a farm, the kitchen garden at Castle Top was another matter. Although even there 'a spectacular root of red cowslips, which my father had propagated himself from a cowslip root,' was settled for its perennial life. 'There were no weeds, for somebody weeded it with great thoroughness, and it was not the children of the house.' Thus such wild flowers that were allowed in lost their stigma or separateness from garden flowers.

Colette, walking back to Manor Farm from school, would find Sido on her knees in that lovely, holy garden described in *Earthly Paradise*, but was not set to toil herself. Sido was wise. She knew that children hate gardening but could be enchanted by gardens. Give them a bit of soil in order to be possessive. Give them a little casual instruction. They will work at their plots but not for you. Alison Uttley was given a plot in which to collect as many stones as plants. Aged ten, my first garden was a rockery underneath greengage trees. Being Suffolk, it could not contain a single rock, only huge flints which had been dragged out of the fields by the plough and cast to the edge. I also remember brick sunflowers and other entablature from an abandoned brickworks nearby, and concrete crazy paving. Penny packets of annuals were sown in May. My brother, whose plot ran with mine under the greengages, grew so many nasturtiums that they ran up the trees. We set our bounds using half-hoops of willow which sprouted in the spring. I can't remember who must have told us about such fences, but fresh graves in the churchyard would sometimes be willowed in this manner until they had settled.

Colette longed for everybody to hear her mother cry 'Look!' It was in this Burgundian farm garden that the pair of them first fell in love with flowers, Colette the novelist-to-be, and Madame Colette, the Parisian widow who had been carried off to the country by a dashing captain.

'In her garden my mother had a habit of addressing to the four cardinal points not only direct remarks and replies that sounded, when heard from our sitting room, like brief inspired soliloquies, but the actual manifestations of her courtesy, which generally took the form of plants and flowers. But in addition to these points – to Cebe and the rue des Vignes, to

Mother Adolphe, and Mâitre de Fourolles – there was also a zone of collateral points, more distant and less defined, whose contact with us was by means of stifled sounds and signals. My childish pride and imagination saw our house as the central point of a mariner's chart of gardens, winds and rays of light, no section of which lay quite beyond my mother's influence.

'. . . I'm really very worried. I can't remember whether it was a family of crocus bulbs I planted there, or the chrysalis of an emperor moth.'

'We've only got to scratch to find out.'

'A swift hand stopped mine. Why did no one ever model or paint or carve that hand of Sido's, tanned and wrinkled early by household tasks, gardening, cold water, and the sun . . .?'

More garden looking goes on in the spring than at any other season. Some years ago I was in the Yonne during May and very near to where Sido made her garden, and peering through lilac-locked iron gates like hers while bells for the Ascension jangled from Vezelay. In Suffolk the lawn-mowers would have been in full concert. My farm garden at Bottengoms has few lawns as such, but many wide grass paths, the broadest alongside the tall orchard grass. I call it the Long Walk and cut it against a swaying wilderness of blossoms, cow parsley, buttercups and fritillaries. A dozen sky-scraping oaks canopy it on the other side. On 21 April 1787 Gilbert White wrote,

'Mowed the grass-walks in part: they were crisp with hoar frost. Cut some grass in the orchard for the horses.'

In May 1793 he was still being tidy. 'My weeding woman swept-up on the grass plot a bushel-basket of blossoms from the white-apple tree; and yet that tree seems still covered with bloom.'

During the early spring of 1942 James Lees Milne saw that

'Francis has been mowing the lawns round the house with the motor tractor, leaving the dead grass lying there, so that there is a heavenly amber-sweet smell of hay, as in midsummer. I wish there were some more wild flowers here besides the dandelions, which I love and others disdain. I lay on the grass and peered closely into the head of one. It was like looking into the inmost recesses of the sun, aswirl with petal flames alive and licking into each other. To think that each of the million dandelions in Buckinghamshire, which are taken for granted or ignored, is in fact a marvellous star of golden beauty. How blind human beings are to the best around them.'

In May 1918 Virginia Woolf was with her sister Vanessa at the recently discovered haven of Charleston, the garden there still in the making.

'I lay with my window open listening to a nightingale, which beginning in the distance came very near the garden. Fishes splashed in the pond. May in England is all they say – so teeming, amorous and creative.'

But Geoffrey Grigson had become pessimistic to the national response to the passionate nature of the seasons and said, 'I think in England we came somewhere near such seasonable observances as moon-viewing or viewing orchards in flower, such a classification, a ritualisation of sensual enjoyment, a hundred and twenty years ago, in the wake of our romanticism, only then it was too late.'

But is it? I don't myself believe so. Obey Sido. Look intimately at what usually escapes your glance. Let it engage the senses.

SUMMER

Gardens are for listening as well as looking. I am reminded of this when more time is spent out of doors than in – when in fact the farmhouse becomes a minor accessory to what surrounds it. Even at night, when my bed seems to be as much outside as in, because of all the windows being wide, it is the garden which encloses me, not the room. It is chiefly because of garden noises. They are especially and welcomingly intrusive in July, the tell-tale movements of unseen creatures, the cry of owls – so many of them at Bottengoms – and the delicious sound of trees caught in the lightest of warm winds. Combined, they produce a wild kind of comfort. The building itself is fully occupied once more. Not just by me but by sparrow, tits and martins bringing up irritable families under the tiles. Now and then I hear Max the cat snoring in the flowers below, and this after he has snoozed on hot flagstones all day. All these night-garden cries, murmurations and flutterings come gift-wrapped in the scents which darkness releases. Like Omar Khayyam, I imagine I hear roses spilling to the earth, and if I listen hard I do hear plops which are only a degree above silence itself.

Bottengoms is so remote from the road and the village that its garden would at first hearing appear free of all contemporary din. But then I realise that although there are the usual aircraft, tractor and distant traffic hummings, I have learned how to edit them out as I convince myself that I am inhabiting a pocket of the old silence. But such noise is so low and muted that visitors never hear it and are occasionally made quite uncomfortable by what they dub 'the peace.' Now and then a neighbour's Amy Johnson-ish plane crackles over, which some find the limit, but which reminds me of childhood and the excitement of catching a glimpse of the pilot's helmeted head, and of pictures in storybooks where those looking up were rewarded with loop the loops and a wave. Cobalt skies. But I suppose it is odd that these Sunday fliers should have a grandstand view of me below. Should I write to the airstrip and ask the names of these people who are always dropping in? Do they like my lay-out? Do they know that they raise the PND (perceived noise decibel) of my birdsong?

Birds certainly are the garden's main sound-makers. Edit them out and what sound remained would be uncanny. Due to the woodlands which surround the garden, and due to the Stour and its water-meadows, springs and contributaries, birdsong and bird-flight noises could not be more various or incessant. There used to be nightingales but now I have to make do with thrushes and blackbirds. At dusk blackbirds fill the indistinct shrubs with their worried tchink-tchink, to be followed by a broken music and a petering out. At this moment the geese from the Grove reservoir whirr across in a thrilling chevron, making for a night on the river. I hesitate to walk through the orchard in case I send up roosting pheasants. Their panic is so catching. I'm sorry, I'm sorry!

As with the nightingales, the work-sounds of others have vanished. If a hoe clinks against a flint, it will be mine. But I can remember lying low and listening to 'the whistling scythes.' Andrew Marvell not only described garden bliss but allows a mysterious character named Damon the Mower to inveigh against the whole business of gardening. Damon believes that just as a garden is a distorted version of nature, so those who confine themselves in them risk a distorted spirit. Distorted back, maybe, say I. Marvell was then living in a great north country house whose grounds, though lovely, kept the real world at a distance. Reading his strangely fascinating mower poems, I think of those distinctive summer sounds which, through the centuries, spoke of keeping the grass in order. Both in lawns and hay-meadows alike, the sound was once the same, the rhythmic swish of the scythe, the rustle of stems falling to the blade, the little screams as whetstone honed steel. In *The Mower Against Gardens,* Damon laments

> *'Tis all enforced, the fountain and the grot,*
> *While the sweet fields do lie forgot.*

Though not by me. The sweet fields which billow up round Bottengoms substantially contribute to its garden sounds. Full-grown wheat can have a noise like the sea. Grazing creatures tear and gulp their food. On Saturday afternoons football or cricket cries filter through and on practise nights, bells clash straight in, loud or thin, according to the breeze. And there is singing along the wires, the first ethereal sound a country child hears, ear clamped to pole, this and its exquisite counterpart when ear is held to shell. The other summer's day I checked on both and there they still were, the conche on the window-sill relaying the Pacific shore, the telegraph post in the track humming away.

The difficulty in trapping garden sounds onto the page is that they tend to take flight from words. John Keats came nearest to capturing the high ceaseless whispering, pulsating susurration which acts as a backing to voices and machines. His disease kept him very much outside and the Hampstead gardens became for him a kind of orchestrated air. It is during summer that I now and then try to cut out words and wheels just to listen to this air. Sprawling on the warm ground, my book curling under the sun, I do a bit of Higher Listening, tuning-in to the soft hubbub made by poplars, the waterfall, bees, the passage of a mouse and to tall plants encountering the wind. Meditation would be a grand word for such listening. The old day-dreaming more like, and sloth certainly. All I am doing is getting the drift of what the garden is saying. A fellow artist would make John Constable lie on his back under a tree and stare at the segments of pure blue through the leaves until he was mesmerised. 'There you are, my dear friend, it is all glazing, all glazing!' But Constable was reading Luke Howard's *The Climate of London* a revolutionary treatise on weather, and what he saw – and heard – was a meeting between land and air. It has never been a silent encounter.

AUTUMN

The year is before itself, as we used to say. A great stretch of sunshine brought an early harvest and, with mostly everything cut by mid-August, autumn arrived with less than ever of its old panache. By late September corn and barley, and many of the summer-autumn bridging flowers, had become a distant memory. Autumn proper indeed will be on its way out before the traditional decay takes over the garden. In which case I will have to wait almost until winter to see whether the high crippled limbs of my oaks are any nearer to falling. Half-wrenched by the 1987 gale, it looks as though they will be able to conceal themselves in foliage until getting on for Christmas. In the strong winds of a normal autumn I would hear them swinging dead and making little screams. Although they thought nothing of slaughtering a whole wood to make a farmhouse or a ship, the demise of standing trees awed our predecessors. That these oaks will soon shed boughs as well as leaves is quite a thought.

'The autumn always gets me badly,' confessed D. H. Lawrence. On the contrary, the autumn always gets me going. A card headed 'To be Done' is tackled with zest. Both the running-down of the light and of vegetable growth for me act as a stimulus. All the stops are out when the days pull in. Besides, I love its smell, its unique rotting musky sweetness and keenness. Where the garden is concerned I have a tendency to get too far ahead and I have to stop myself from hurrying the clearances along. Decay must take its time, or how else can it happen?

John Nash taught me the aesthetics of decomposition, that rotting is a part of life, that leaves should blacken and seeds should rattle. What greater delight than to find a patch of cyclamen in rich pink blooms in a wispy thicket of brittle stalks, or a late rose, ditto? All the leaves appear to rustle from the grapevine at noon sharp on one particular day, exposing nests and all kinds of litter. It must not be pruned until December or else it bleeds. Should there be storms it will beat against its orange wall and I shall listen to it whilst lying a foot or two from it in my bed. 'That's the vine,' I will say. Harold has turned its fruit into wine, and has labelled it Vin Bottengoms 1996. It is sharp, refreshing and intoxicating. 'You'll have to watch your step all right!'

I scythe the nettles in the wild with a new blade and an ancient haft, and ask myself why I had endured a bent and notched cutting-edge for so long. The new one slides through the stinging forest, laying it flat. Very soon a soft nettle lawn with edible tips will appear Our derision when mother made a nettle soup and our silence when it tasted so good! They say that this aggravating plant stowed itself away with the seed-corn which the East Anglians took to Massachusetts in the 1630s. These first Americans declared it to be 'the first Plant taken notice of' there. Nettles like to grow where men have lived. It flourishes so mightily in the wastes of Bottengoms that I have long given up attempting to cope with it and simply let it rip. Now that broad-leafed trees have been planted where the elms died, an old farmer friend and myself now and then tread a circle of nettles to death around them.

The first autumns of these youthful trees, oak, chestnut, maple, I find very moving. Their bright leaves whirl by in the early stages of a deciduous ritual which will continue long after I have disappeared. The elm boles sprout a few shoots which won't come to much, and badgers, foxes and rabbits have scraped sandy paths around them. Mixed with mown nettle and trodden nettle there is the occasional whiff of animal, raw and unmistakable. Here and there I have to lift the scythe in order to save my beloved red campion, so liked in fact that it is allowed to thrive in the flower-beds. They called it Poor Jane in Suffolk. In autumn it makes healthy hummocks amongst all the dead and dying, and there isn't a day in the year when it is not in flower somewhere. It possessed randy meanings for the Elizabethans although, as with similarly suggestive properties for so many of their plants, I never quite knew why. I should have asked Cedric Morris; he was very sexy in gardens, bringing one's attention to a disgraceful botany. He and the Elizabethans certainly found gardens very merry in ways which escaped me.

Autumn is formally announced at Bottengoms by the overnight appearance of purple and white *colchicum speciosum*. Suddenly they are there, naked and flawless, amidst plants spotty with age. One clump has bloomed on clay for years and I am baffled that anything so unprotectedly white and gleaming should rise immaculately there, for the ground is dried hard after the summer, and sticky when it rains. But the autumn flower when we were children was Michaelmas Daisy, every species of which made huge bushes in village gardens, usually tied up with string against a wall, and covered with old lace curtains when it was frosty. On Mondays we took it to school, this and asters. There they stood in stone jars on the window-sills until their stems grew rank – an autumn reek of truly Proustian significance. Is it my fancy, but are there far fewer Michaelmas Daisies now? They were not much thought of by country folk then but were celebrated for 'coming in handy' when everything else was 'going off.' They dominated harvest festivals.

Autumn is rarely what autumn says. It has more warmth and sun than has been popularly allowed it. And yet it is inescapably senescent, hence its poignancy. It is sweet-smelling of corruption and is full of departures. So why does it wake me up? I plan, I start a new book, I look eagerly ahead when I should be looking back, and I am excited. Just ahead is winter and autumn should be saying, like Harold with the wine, 'Watch out!' Yet it is also telling me in a sumptuous language something about maturity, and about all of us being in the same boat as the plants which, when one comes to think of it, is a pretty unsinkable boat once one has accepted the reality that seeds have to die in order to live.

A fine new stove has arrived to burn the gale wood in and my eye begins to fall on special books for winter nights. All the fruit is in jam-jars or the deep freeze, or regimented on shelves: blackberries, apples, quince, pears, plums. The mower has been put away after the last cut but I have to wait for ages before the last leaves are down and the last clean-up. Flora Thompson said, 'Laggard to come laggard to go' – the oaks of course. East Anglian autumns usually end in violence, or what the poet John Clare called wind 'spirits in their startling moods.' The garden which had been so warm and still- 'We are still having breakfast outside', boasts a neighbour – has suddenly grown tempestuous and cold. It is saying, What do you expect? You have made me in a river valley. Which is why it becomes Chinese. Along in the lane, massed walls of mist where there is usually a clear view of Stoke-by-Nayland. A dripping silence which makes me pull the curtains. Gaudiness giving way to colourlessness. When everything is all but gone, I make a little count of what is 'still out.' Then I give up because there are so many. Always red campion, always a rose.

WINTER

I hear people say that, due to some streak of mildness in the weather, or a determined blindness to it on their part, they 'hardly noticed the winter.' Here and gone it was before one could say blast. And barely a hint of desolation. Which I have always thought a pity. No gardener should think of trying to dodge winter, or observe its harsh antics with dismay. It is rest time for the gardener, who can ignore to some degree 'what has to be done in January' manuals. Not much can be done in January except keep warm, eat well, read much, admire ice and snow in their season, smell old rooms in which hyacinths have spent the night and walk at a spanking pace. Old books give out some funny old opinions. In one of them Elizabeth von Arnim says that she finds the scent of hyacinths 'wanting in chastity.'

Arum lilies perhaps, but not hyacinths. Let us not place this perfume anywhere but in a winter's room, and as incense for our post-Christmas rites.

> *If thou of fortune be bereft,*
> *And in thy store there be but left*
> *Two loaves – sell one, and with the dole*
> *Buy hyacinths to feed thy soul.*

For Countess Elizabeth they are a 'smell', a winter make-do in that cold castle, because 'in winter one cannot be fastidious.' Joachim wandered in to Poland to find the remnants of her German garden, the big house gone but its terraces and grounds still traceable on the bitter acres. There is a snapshot of the young English tutor E. M. Forster sitting there. Joachim brings me more photographs of the site now. All that famous planting, and now nothing. Not so, he tells me. Is he not a celebrated recoverer of old gardens? Can he not see what was there? Her hyacinths apart, the Countess relished and understood the purposes of a great garden in winter – none better. Those were the days when the cold of indoors made the cold of outdoors no more than a variation of cold, and when one dressed for the entrance hall. Thus at Nassenheide, her Pomeranian schloss, both garden and house were for her united in their wintriness And as they were such for three frozen months every year, she was obliged to be positive about it. She stayed inside then, planning plantings and usually got so carried away with catalogues from England that when it came to ordering things such as marrow-seed and primrose roots, marvellous quantities would arrive of species unknown to 1898 Prussia. What with her ice-locked soil, and what with her asides on hyacinths, etc. one can still experience the flavour of Nassenheide in January. The little tutor from Cambridge would have stamped about and flailed his arms to keep his circulation going. E. M. Forster was making notes.

'Don't you get snowed in?' I am asked by visitors to low-lying Bottengoms. Of course, now and then. When one lives in a hollow snow naturally fills it up, and although at first stunned by its quiet immensity and beauty, I soon set my 'drift' routine into motion. I check that I can get up to the lane via the high field, which is often thin on the top, like an old man's head, and that the paraffin lamp is full and plenty of logs are in, for the power and telephone lines now hang in thick white ropes. Then I release shrubs from their intolerable burden of snow-platters before boughs snap, then I ring the village shop which will tell the world that I am All Right, and please leave letters, Felix, human food and whatever usually comes down to the house, in a box by a wall about a mile away. Then I tell myself, as the prophet told himself, that this, like all things, is only for a time. Confessing these practices to an American friend on a summer's day, he recommended that I should read a poem by John Green-leaf Whittier entitled *Snowbound.* I did and thought it the finest description ever of the subject. The poet was a boy at the time and was cooped up with his family at Haverhill Massachusetts and, as fate would have it, two difficult women who were just visiting when it began to snow. It was the winter of 1866. It struck me that one should either be with a lover or quite alone in a house which is drift-locked.

Really epic winters are thin on the ground these days, though regularly forecast. The garden at Bottengoms only disappears in bi-decadal blizzards. For the most part it retains, January after January, its stark visibility, becoming open and spacious, like familiar old rooms when their clutter is removed or tidied away, and their simple lineaments are revealed. I can look through beds and hedges instead of into them and revel in a land of sticks. Quite a few daisies are out in the sodden grass. Premature digging will sometimes uproot a bulb and I can be taken aback by the vigour of its white and green growth. Winter is all hard dissolution on the surface and tender vitality below it. I may loaf – it is a great reading time – but the garden does not, for a moment. Our piercing winds tear through it and the cold can be unspeakable. There are days when no one goes outside. Yet through a window I can see the hellebores looking quite comfortable and, on my neighbour's field, fresh corn as bright as a button and quite unbuffeted. Keeping off the frozen grass takes me on unusual garden walks. I see where frost creates an absolute stillness. Shorn trees are immersed in their yearly drill of not stirring; never so much as a tremor to reveal their busy inner greening. Not so, of course, *Garrya elliptica* (named after young Michael Garry of the Hudson Bay Company) whose catkin cascades and dense, tough leaves make such a nice contrast against the snow.

I am rarely depressed by winter at its worst. I remember lines like John Crowe Ransom's 'A cry of Absence, Absence, in the heart/And in the wood the furious winter blowing,' and tell myself, Yes, Yes! Bleakness can be blissful, as can all extremes. Hoping to find an artefact on the Stone Age village site, my gaze screwed to the mud, I appreciate the terror into which the old settlers tumbled after the winter solstice, having no guarantee that the summer would come again. This would have been in February, after they had eaten everything up and shivered among the flints. Hunger is very lowering, very black. Good gardeners prepare themselves for the worst as well as for the best.

Still may you with your frozen fingers cut
Treasures of Winter, if you planted well;
The Winter-sweet against a sheltering wall,
Waxen, Chinese and drooping bell;
Strange in its colour, almond in its smell
And the Witch-hazel, Hamamelis mollis,
That comes before its leaf on naked bough,
Torn ribbons frayed of, yellow and maroon,
And sharp of scent in frosty English air . . .
Gardener, if you listen, listen well:
Plant for your winter pleasure, when the months
Dishearten . . .

(Vita Sackville West, *The Garden*)

Solvitur Ambulando:
John Clare and Footpath Walking

None of us now realise what walking was like to Clare and his contemporaries in villages such as Helpston. In what remains a unique study of such parochial travels, *The English Path* (1979), Kim Taplin wonders why this, one of the main routes to our literature, particularly our poetry, has received so little investigation. There are shelves full of books on roads but one would have to search hard for something on paths. In fact, the study of paths is as fugitive as many of the paths themselves. One of her chapters is headed *Solvitur Ambulando*, which she translates as 'you can sort it out by walking.' And indeed you can.

'Working out, finding out, unknotting and freeing are all possible connotations of the word *solvitur*, and in this chapter I want to look at the claims of certain writers for the benefits of footpath walking to the spirit. Andrew Young used the words in his poem *A Traveller in Time*:

> *Where was I? What was I about to see?*
> Solvitur ambulando.
> *A path offered its company.*

A companionable path was more apt for a curative release than a road, since solitude, pace and close contact with nature, as well as the action of walking, are all important ingredients. Problems unravel as the feet cover the miles, but through the body's surroundings, as well as the body's action.'

My own existence is still as controlled by footpaths as those of my Suffolk ancestors. Friends never tire of telling me that my life would be transformed if only I could drive a car, quite forgetting how transformed it has been because I cannot. And so each day I walk a mile or so of flinty track to fetch the milk, and each week two miles or so to the post office, church and pub, and more miles still when my thoughts run out and the typewriter clicks to a halt, and I have to wander off to the river paths for a little *solvitur ambulando*. And so I have done since boyhood in these more or less same scenes. And so indeed did all our forebears, including some quite recent ones. And did we but know it, many of our best poems, stories and essays smell not of the lamp, but of dust, mud, grit, pollen and sweat. Even the clergy understood *solvitur ambulando* and planted 'sermon walks'. There was a nice one at Little Easton Rectory where I used to stay as a youth, a lengthy lawn set between discreet yew hedges along which the priest could stroll and spin thoughts around his text.

John Clare is the genius of the footpath. So poignant is his statement on the Great North Road that it tends to overlay his happy and myriad statements on footpaths. That wretched journey in July 1841, just after his forty sixth birthday, when he was even more alone than he thought he was, his dream-wife all unbeknown to him having died, starving, penniless, blood in his broken shoes, is the walk which has obliterated all his previous tracks. He had, he said 'lay down with my head towards the north to show myself the steering point in the morning'. This was a walk entirely isolated from every other walk he had made, or would ever make. Yet during the nineteenth century – or during any century other than our own – to tramp eighty miles along one of Britain's main highways in daily stages was commonplace. Enormous distances were covered by William and Dorothy Wordsworth, by Coleridge and the Hazlitts –

especially Mrs Hazlitt, one of the proto new women. Her ceaseless hikes to and fro between Edinburgh and Glasgow during her divorce proceedings were a tremendous nuisance to those having to carry them out. Gustav Holst liked to walk back from St Paul's Girls' School, Hammersmith to Cheltenham in order to compose. William Langland wrote much of *Piers Plowman* on the hoof from Cornhill, London to the Malvern Hills where he was born. Had John Clare been the sturdy man he was before disasters of all kinds struck him, being an inspired walker, he would have been neither spiritually daunted nor physically hurt by his 'Journey out of Essex.' But then he would not have needed to make it.

Clare's true life's journey was via Helpston's footpaths. His misfortune was to watch these being either ploughed up or straightened out. A large part of his personality was as concealment-seeking as that of the nightingale and as hopefully hidden as that of certain tucked-away plants on the Barnack limestone. The remainder of him was the same as that of most young countrymen, gregarious, fond of a particular kind of company, fond of drink, fond of girls. It was the Clare of the footpaths and their fugitive destinations, their hidden bends, where he could 'drop down', as he said, to write or simply daydream, and whose soul was fed by what so closely surrounded him, who produced the poetry. He was clearly unaware of how frequently he mentions footpaths and his essentially secret wanderings, most of them no more than a stone's throw of Helpston's various labouring and playing groups. Some of his finest footpath writing is in an essay entitled *The Woodman, or Beauties of a Winter's Forest* Here Clare observes his footpath-walking neighbours as they journey all exposed on the bleak land. Summer's cover has been all stripped away.

'the shepherd cuts his journeys short and now only visits his flock on necessity ... Croodling with his hands in his pockets and his crook under his arm he tramples the frosty plain with dithering haste, glad and eager to return to the warm corner of his cottage fire ... The Milk-boy too in his morning rambles no longer saunters to the pasture as he had used to do in summer pausing on every pathway flower and swanking idly along, often staring with open-mouth thoughtless musing on the heavens as if he could wish for something in the passing clouds, leaning his lazy sides 'gainst every stile he comes to, and can never get his heavy clouted shoon over the lowest without resting, sighing as he retires with the deepest regret to leave such easy chairs. But now in hasty claumping tread finding nothing but cold and snow to pause on ... he wishes for nothing but his journey's end.'

In March that same year, 1825, Clare's own footpath presented sights more vigorous, less frozen and with a livelier lad to share it. It is difficult for us to comprehend how peopled the old countryside was. I can just remember it as a Suffolk child, the path with another occupant suddenly hoving into view, the brushing past and the muttered greeting. Now I can walk the six mile round from the farmhouse and back again with not a single encounter. In grandfather's time the paths were all little toiling highways. Hedgers with their hooks slashing away, ditchers looking up and out, children playing and on Sundays solemn processions of walks finely and unsuitably dressed filling in the hours between family lunch and high tea. Now and then lovers would appear in the long grass, soft and dishevelled like nesting birds, their faces kept hidden, their tangled bodies quite still and we looked 'without looking', hungry for what they offered. On 25th March 1825 John Clare went flower-hunting.

'I took a walk today to botanize and found that the spring had taken up her dwelling in good earnest. She has covered the woods with the white anemone which the children call Lady smocks and the hare bells are just venturing to unfold their blue drooping bells. The green is covered with daisies and the little Celandine. The hedge bottoms are crowded with the green leaves of the arum where the boy is peeping with pootys with eager anticipation and delight.'

Though most of our footpaths follow their original purpose, which was to make beelines across farmland or over moors or over cliffs, they are either deserted or protected, or threatened, or are over-walked by armies of ramblers so that they, delicate trails for local feet, break up under the heavy tread. Multitudes of them spider across local maps but are no longer local knowledge. Some have widened into lanes, and the lanes into roads. A lane is defined as a narrow way between hedges and banks. A footpath is the narrowest way which can be trodden between crops or wild plants. John Clare mourned the loss of many of his narrowest ways when they enclosed Helpston. He raged and ranted about it justly, recognising the sacrilege of destroying one of the holiest places in any community, the paths towards work, towards marriage, towards vision, paths which were infinitely precious to man, woman and child.

I was once taken by a friend to John Bunyan's footpaths. We walked to a rough little spot by the side of a rivulet where his father's house had stood and which had served the Bunyans for generations. We saw a few tiles amongst the weeds. The absolute disappearance of the great Walker's house excepted, his home fields around Elstow must be among the least changed surroundings of any major topographical writer. To this day they can be reached only by the footpaths which Bunyan trod, one of which follows the stream from Harrowden, the other taking us into the heart of his allegory. And – shades of John Clare – a local clergyman had noted in 1625, when Bunyan himself was three, so it could not have been him, the 'one Bunion of Elstow, climbing of rooks' nests in the Berry Wood, found three rooks in a nest, all as white as milk, and not a black feather in them.'

Footpaths did not guarantee solitude. We make a mistake in thinking that John Clare simply by walking out of Helpston found seclusion. There was always somebody up a tree or spread under a bush, somebody tiffling about, as they said, with a scythe or a hook, sweethearts in the long grass, children at their games and workers routinely plodding from home to job. Footpaths could be busy by day and not empty at night. So those who needed no interruption struck off from them into private hinterlands and would make a waste their realm. Bunyan, a whitesmith humping an anvil, sensibly kept to the narrow way. But it was not a lonely way.

Though once used by everybody, the footpath proper could only be walked single file, and should you meet someone coming from the opposite direction you would step into the undergrowth to let them pass. Such constant narrow treading stimulated the wild flowers which in summer separated only just far enough to allow human feet to journey on. Similarly there were ground nests perilously close to the path. The ghostly footpaths of winter came into their own during the snowy Christmas of 1928 when the writer Adrian Bell noted how, the lanes being blocked by drifts, villagers returned to their old useful tracks. From his farmhouse in the Stour Valley he observed them walking directly across the thinly snowed fields to where they had to go, their eyes fixed on a spire or a chimney or some guiding tree. 'And who are they? Not travellers from afar, for they would not venture out today at all. No, these are the parish workers who, when times are normal, take serpentine routes by by-roads on bicycles.'

'Take the gentle path,' advises George Herbert in his plea 'Discipline.' Bunyan insisted that the only way to become a heavenly footman – he means a walker in paradise, not a servant – was to make the commuting distance between home and work a pilgrim-way. Until recently, few had any alternative but to foot it every day to the job. Clare's constant walking to and from the mill and then the field, and then the lime-kiln, was the norm. But as well as walking to gardening, hedging, ploughing and on errands, he would walk to what was to his neighbours plainly not work, to reading and writing and dreaming in hollows and woods, a very odd thing to do – and especially as he did it so often. Often he would walk off the footpath just to look! And so before he was out of his teens he became what most country folk dread being – strange, different, not really one of them. With so many of Helpston's hereditary footpaths destroyed, ironed-out or exposed by enclosure, the young poet would find himself having to walk out of the ruin of the old known ways and into the peripheral wilds. These were wonderful. It was there he made gypsy-friends and sat in long-abandoned workplaces such as Roman settlements and the open-cast quarry at Barnack where an army of medieval masons had chiselled-out churches and cathedrals. The 'Hills and Holes' of Barnack, its limestone acres thick with rare flowers, was a naturalist's dream to which he had his own special right of way.

John Clare often writes of 'dropping down' when he needed to make notes, a kind of birdlike movement when a thought struck him. When he was working as a lime-burner, he had to walk between two kilns which were about three miles apart, one at Pickworth and the other at Ryhall. At Pickworth he worked with another man, at Ryhall by himself. He wrote 'I often went there to work by myself, where I had leisure over such things on my journeys of going and returning to and fro; and on these walks morning and night I have dropped down 5 or 6 times to write.'

There was no dropping down when he was ploughing, which would have been a very public thing to do. What came to him in the open fields he had to hold tight in his head until he reached his bedroom. Then he would write. Whilst at work he would 'mutter' as he called his memorizing process, the lines he would put on paper at the end of the day. And hard come-by paper at that. In his autobiography *Sketches in the Life of John Clare* he uses the walk metaphor to describe his early sense of being different and isolated from those around him. His illiterate mother had talked of his going into service and had given him a box to contain his clothes etc. when he left home. But he had filled it with books and his first poems.

'I always looked sullen when my other talked of service . . . I now began to value my abilities as superior to my companions and exalted over it in secret . . . I considered walking in the track of others but this had as little merit in it as a child walking in leading strings ere it can walk by itself. When I happened with them (his companions) in my Sunday walks I often tried their taste by pointing out some striking beauty in a wild flower or object in the surrounding scenery to which they would seldom make an answer, and if they did 'twas such as "they could see nothing worth looking at . . ." I often wondered that, while I was peeping about and finding such quantities of pleasing things to stop and pause over, another should pass me as careless as if he was blind. I thought sometimes that I had surely had a taste peculiarly by myself and that nobody else thought or saw things as I did.'

They did not, of course – that is, not until Clare had turned such observations into poems, and then they did. But 'peeping', 'secret', 'seeing', 'finding', this is the language of the footpath walker. Clare's very first poem was entitled *The Morning Walk* and was composed whilst walking the two miles to Glinton. Years later, when he was working on the great book that never was, his Helpston version of Gilbert White's *Natural History of Selborne*, he remembered a marvellous sight from a footpath, and wrote,

'Once, when I was a young man, on staying late at a feast, I crossed a meadow about midnight and saw to my surprise quantities of small nimble things emigrating across it a long way from any water. I thought at first that they were snakes, but I found on a closer obser-vation that they were young eels making for a large pond called the Islet pool, which they journeyed to with as much knowledge as if they were acquainted with the way. I thought this a wonderful dis-covery.'

Clare was himself more than just acquainted with the way, that simplest, purest, most eloquent of ways, the footpath. And life only went wrong when he was diverted from it. He knew where he stood. He knew where he should walk. He knew where he should drop down. He knew what no other English writer knew or knows, which is what rural English eyes saw, and still see, an indigenous landscape in all its reality. He was hard on the ' clowns', as he called them, those locals who some-how never manage to see a thing, but we know that countless people on the way to work, or at work itself, are unwittingly visionary. What they do not do is to drop down in the familiar tracks in order to write what they see or feel, not having the writer's compunction or skill.

There were days when Clare himself was unable to walk. On Thursday 23 September 1824, he confessed,

A wet day. Did nothing but nurse my illness. Could not have walked out had it been fine. Very disturbed in conscience about the troubles of being forced to endure life and die by inches and the anguish of leaving my children and the dark porch of eternity whence none returns to tell the tale of their reception.

But a few weeks later – what a change!

Sunday 31 Oct 1824
Took a walk. Got some branches of the spindle tree with its pink coloured berries that shine beautifully in the pale sun – found for the first time 'the herb true love', or 'one berry' (Paris quatrifolia) in Oxey Wood. Brought a root home to set in my garden.

The following spring there were endless footpath walks, one at three o'clock in the morning, and one that ended up with the comic scene of the poet barking like a dog in order to see off a vixen (13 May 1825):

Met with an extraordinary incident today while walking in open wood to hunt a nightingale's nest – I popped unawares on an old Fox and her four young cubs that were playing about, she saw me and instantly approached towards me growling like an angry dog. I had no stick and tried all I could to fright her by imitating the bark of a fox hound which only irritated her the more and if I had not retreated a few paces back she would have seized me when I set up an haloo she started.

Clare had all the countryman's terror of spooks, of shadows, of following footsteps, of fierce animals:

> *The boy returning home at night from toil*
> *Down lane and close o'er footbrig gate and style*
> *Oft trembles into fear and stands to hark*
> *The waking fox renew his short gruff bark*
> *While badgers echo their dread evening shrieks*
> *And to his thrilling thoughts in terror speaks*
> (The Shepherd's Calendar)

Margaret Grainger, the editor of *The Natural History Prose Writings of John Clare*, an astonishing work, speaks of some of the poet's walks being systematic. Whilst he mostly wandered, there were days when he walked to plan. She traces three such walks, one due east from Northborough to the River Welland and along the west bank to Deeping Gate; one from Nine Bridges, Northborough and then to Lolham Bridges via the North Drain, and one between Waldram Hall and Welland Ford. These systematic walks were taken with the discipline of the naturalist. Dr. Grainger also noticed marks on Clare's manuscripts which proved that his natural history notes must indeed have been jotted down as he walked. 'I used to drop down behind a hedge bush or dyke and write down my things upon the crown of my hat.'

Assisting in editing the New Wessex Edition of the Works of Thomas Hardy, I came upon his work methods – writers are always fascinated by other writers' work methods, right down to ink, pens and typewriters. Hardy's were there in all their simplicity in that little room he shared with his brother at Bockhampton. There was the small cupboard where they kept their clothes, and there was the narrow wooden window-seat in the casement on which Hardy sat to write *Far from the Madding Crowd*. The house had been built by his grandfather in a woodland – the woodland of *The Woodlanders* – and when Hardy needed to stretch his legs he would hurry from the cottage and walk where the woodmen were working, making the white chips fly. His brain still racing with the novel, he would pick up the chips and continue with the chapter in pencil, filling his pocket with sentences. Exactly what Clare was doing when he used his hat as a desk.

References to footpath soliloquies and encounters are myriad in both writers. In *Stray Walks* Clare says,

> *How pleasant are the fields to roam and think*
> *Whole sabbaths through, unnoticed and alone*

And there was his ever-sacred walk to Mary Joyce, his spirit wife, the walk he would continue to take in the madhouse. One of the horrible ironies of his existence was that he, the footpath walking countryman par excellence, had to make such journeys in his head instead of on the ground. Once it was the lover's dash to Glinton, Mary's home:

> *I've run the furlongs to thy door*
> *And thought the way as miles*
> *With doubts that I should see thee not*
> *And scarcely staid for stiles*

Then for many years it was the poor old celebrity making his way from the asylum to the porch of Northampton parish church, looking at little en route, all the 'seeing' going on in another place. Clare's footpath masterpiece is *The Pewits Nest*. As one reads it one comes closest to the poetry of every walking man. It moves us because it tells us of our descent from generations of walking men and women, walking children too. It is easy to forget that it was not just the Clares and Hardys and Constables and Wordsworths who saw glory as they walked – who gained ideas, who felt elation. *Solvitur ambulando* was and is for all. Just because most people cannot drop down to paint or write what walking does to the vision of existence, it does not follow that the vision itself is only given to the few. When George Crabbe was writing about his marshy footpaths, his frequently vitriolic account of rural society was given a sudden sweetness by descriptions of fishermen and fieldworkers 'away' from their then despised labours and absorbed in their hobbies. Here were the naturalists whose knowledge of birds, plants and insects would have been revealed in John Clare's *Natural History of Helpston* had not the days darkened for him. Here were the kind of friends he made. We call them self-educated but their true education was something we cannot comprehend. If often went far deeper than the reading of books. It came from the local landscape being articulated in their heads via their normal work practices. They had to work all day and every day. They didn't live as long as we now live yet they often saw things as curiously as poets saw them. The social historian plods along their rough paths. In his great poem *The Pewits Nest* Clare sets out on his quintessential footpath walk:

> *Across the fallow clods at early morn*
> *I took a random track where scant and spare*
> *The grass and nibbled leaves all closely shorn*
> *Leaves a burnt flat all bleaching brown and bare . . .*

Now read on. Now walk on.

Doctor Grace

One's first funeral in the fully understood sense has to be that of a contemporary. Not even that of a parent includes one in the death. My first funeral was that of Harry Shaw, a schoolfriend, who was ten or thereabouts. I suppose I must have attended grandfather's funeral some years before this, but if I did I have retained no memory of it, nothing except a shuffling of footsteps among the leaves. But Harry's funeral still has the clarity of a selected scene locked in a viewfinder. If I think of it I see it exactly. There we all were, his class, and there was Harry in his white coffin and a torrent of white flowers. Preadolescents were always buried virginally. He had died of consumption. So had Lily Ward, whose snowy cortège would soon be following his up the crunchy path. I recall how it was bad enough to know that Harry had 'gone' without having to see where he had gone. Not above the blue sky but down into the deepest, muddiest hole imaginable. Down, down he went, the undertaker's men letting out the white straps for what seemed like an hour whilst the rector shouted prayers into the wind. Such sadness. We, the other boys and myself, were rushed into mortality, something which previously had belonged only to grown-ups and animals. Our black armbands marked us, as trees for felling are marked, for the earth. A day or two later, when we visited his grave, it was to find his existence all smoothed away by turves and fluttering blooms. I thought of his beautiful, flawless consumptive skin in the blackness. Lily's skin was the same, though intensified by the frame of her heavy damp hair which, mother said approvingly, they never cut. Removing long ropes of hair from a sick girl might be cooling, but what would she look like when she was laid out?

'Was it galloping consumption?'

'No -more's the pity.'

Lingering children. Children with names from Victorian tales who were read to by the last of the lamplight and who knew that they would never live to hear the last pages, and all of them as commonplace a part of our experience as the plough horses stumbling up and down the fields.

Harry died in a house which adjoined the public hall where the Dramatic Society performed and where Saturday night dance music throbbed, which made him a rather sophisticated figure in our eyes. Lily died in a terrace house just up from the railway station, listening to the musical couplings of trucks. Everything that could be done had been done for them, they said. Meaning that nothing could be done, other than to keep the windows open. The bitterest Suffolk air available was their medicine. Gales would put back the roses in their cheeks. Their eyes shone like glass. They welcomed us with languid voices and, when we left, lifting their heads from the counterpane, they were like hot silk.

'Can you catch it?' we asked mother.

'Only if it is born into you.'

She meant, I suppose, the inherited factor. There were entire families born into it and when the last member of such a family was borne from the cottage, often no one else would go to live in it because the consumption might be galloping in the wallpaper or in the well. So these blighted dwellings were dubbed by the village pestilential and often left to decay. But usually they were scrubbed to the core with carbolic, and their windows closed.

His funeral apart, my chief memory of Harry Shaw was of us looking for toads in flints. One of the unsolved riddles of Nature was how toads got into flints. So we sat side by side in old gravel pits, hammering away at large flints, making the sparks fly, engrossed by the impending revelation when the two halves should fall apart and the toad, who himself contained a stone, an emerald was the popular belief, should blink at us after his mysterious incarceration. Never a toad, though frequently a nice whirled chamber fit for a toad. Farmwork went on high above our heads. When we tired of toads we turned to newts, which swam in the gravel-pit pond. Captured, they writhed in our jamjars like bewildered dragons. When they said in their knowing way that Harry would never make old bones it meant nothing to me. How could he, so perfect, not live? I wished I looked like him, so marble white.

'Don't say such things!' they said.

Bike rides took my brothers and me to Wissington. There it was the prams, not the disease, which shocked us. No matter for what good reason, it struck us that for grown men to lie outside in huge prams in all weathers, and in full view of passers-by, was one of those cures which were worse than the sickness itself. These consumptives lay in a neat row on a high lawn above the Stour, and they waved and called out cheerily when they caught us staring. A black leatherette apron and hood protected them from the rain. If you could afford if you bought cold weather in Davos or had the 'German cure.' If you could afford nothing, and were fortunate enough 'to be seen' by either Dr. Jane or Dr. Grace, your brief day might be prolonged in the sanatorium near Nayland. This building was – is – architecturally delightful. Dr. Jane and her friend Millicent Fawcett built it in 1898, adding wings and a cupola to it until, when we knew it, just before the last war, it could at night be taken for a little palace, with its hilltop splash of windows and lights. I see it still, facing me across the garden and the valley, a row of houses now, but still with the ghost of that obsolescence which hangs about an outdated hospital. Thirty years earlier, Millicent's sister Elizabeth Garrett Anderson had founded her hospital for women, and to be run by women, in Euston Road. In 1918, a young Welsh doctor, Grace Griffith, exhausted by war work, accepted a fortnight's locum at Millicent's sanitorium in Suffolk – and never left. Dr. Grace, as she was known in our countryside for the next fifty years, was selflessness and commonsense personified. She arrived at the sanatorium in a horse and cart from Bures station but was soon seen dashing through the tortuous lanes on a motorbike. Both Dr. Grace's sister and Mrs. Fawcett's brother had died from tuberculosis, and along with Dr. Jane Walker, after whom the eyrie-like sanatorium was named, so they were emotionally and practically committed to the nursing of consumptives. These were rife in East Anglia, a blowy place where one would not have expected such chokings and dyings, such dread. Older people still favoured the warm cure of the Mediterranean. As a regime it did not insist upon icy bedrooms and lying in prams in the snow.

Consumption, like all the great illnesses, was entirely democratic and the sufferers and their families went through pains, treatments, attitudes and emotions which had received wide coverage in novels, poetry and music. TB with its decline, and its power to create a brief untouchable beauty and a heightened imagination, was one of the more artistic ways to go. It refined as it suffocated. Socially it bore no disgrace, no guilt. It was simply fatal. Aids must be its modern equivalent so far as hopelessness is concerned, but that is all. The newly diagnosed consumptive and those just discovered to be HIV positive are leagues apart in social acceptance and love. Some of the sanatorium patients were driven away to the family vault, others still lie under wooden crosses in the bumpy churchyard a mile or two down the lane. They were paupers. The ladies, as they were known, in dealing with the great commonwealth of the sick, ignored class.

By the mid-nineteen twenties Dr. Grace was involved in her own practice in the valley. Married, with eventually six children, she took over its care during the penury of the agricultural depression. She was tall, plain and smiling, with a faintly drawling, plangent voice, and the formidable yet gentle unorthodoxy of someone who sees that things get done. She had now changed her motorbike for a battered car in which she crammed not only her own children, but those of any farmworker whose wife needed a few days rest after giving birth. Everybody told her everything. Not very long after Harry's death, I told her that I wanted to be a writer, an artist 'or something like that.' It was my first confession, and made when we ran into each other at the local flower show. Long afterwards, when I was middle-aged and she was ancient, she remembered it. She gave up using names early on. When she delivered babies in the cottages there was Mother, Father and Dears. Father will come to the surgery for codliver oil and malt, Mother must rest. Dears would be 'helpful.'

Her parish was redoubtable, daring anyone, let alone a 'lady doctor' to take it on. It began near Dr. Jane's and Dame Millicent's sanatorium and ended many years later as most of West Suffolk. As usual, the worst difficulties, the most pain, the greatest injustice, would lie behind well-nigh impenetrable secrecy and discretion. Dr. Grace heard what it was necessary to hear, not from counselling in today's sense, but accompanying the screams of deliveries, the 'disgrace' of impetigo, the medieval terrors of diphtheria, scarlet fever and other poxes, and slightly from 'worry'. She was masterly on worry. She grew powerful, influential. A sharp note to some laggard authority put the fear of God into it. By the 1930s to disobey Dr. Grace, who *was* always right, and most decidedly always kind, was something no one would like to be made public. She herself taught Mother birth control behind Father's back. She rescued bright children from serfdom and, though extremely untidy herself, brought order to squalid dwellings. She told her patients things they were surprised to hear and which they found hard to forget. The long hours and scanty money, and her own six children, the endless calls in all weathers, the health checks at the packed schools, made her majestically gaunt, pared-down, but never fragile. The plaintive, sad, off-key voice, rather like that of certain calling birds, made the cottage door fly open.

In 1927, she herself hired a cottage on Tiger Hill, placing by its side what looked suspiciously like one of Dr. Jane's huts from which to watch nature. The lonely cottage and green shed were a hide in every sense of the word. It concealed her from the Tiger Hill creatures, from the ever-demanding inhabitants of the valley, and from, perhaps, Dr. David her husband, an amiable drinking man who held court in little inns. 'Has Doc been in yet?' Everyone hoped that he hadn't for it meant that the night was young. I remember as a youth, Doc, the poet W. R. Rodgers and myself trying to reach some pub in dense fog, Doc driving inch by inch along the road verge which, branching off, lost us in no time at all. So there we sat, trapped by Bertie Rodgers' soft Irish storytelling as well as the creamy-black fog and its wraith hands fingering the windscreen. Doc rarely mentioned Dr. Grace or she him. Chalk and cheese, everybody said, though I have come to doubt it. Those who could not recognise tolerance in marriage were divided between being sorry for her or sorry for him. Each was alarmingly unselfish.

Tiger Hill, Dr. Grace's hide, was a mile or two from Dr. Jane's sanatorium, and was part of the wood named Arger Fen. The Tiger Hill land and the Arger Fen land was separated by a steep lane which descended and rose from a watersplash. It enthralled us as children because it was a kind of forest village, a real 'woodlanders' home, with houses and gardens tucked away in its shade, and ground marks where for centuries a little community, dominated by trees, had made a living. The tiger of Dr. Grace's hill was allegedly a sabre-toothed tiger. Tusks and teeth from the chalk below the gravel-pit workings were crammed into the school museum, along with models of Calvary, Saxon coins and stuffed birds, living examples of whose species sat feeding in the winter fields in their hundreds. Dr. Grace received our visits to Tiger Hill as she would have received grown-ups, without admitting tiredness. But we remained in awe of her, as one should of a legend. Like the consumptives, she was stretched out in the air and the sun. Like them, she waved a thin arm when she glimpsed us. Far from the Lysol and worn Mothers, she watched the Tiger Hill badgers and listened to the nightingales. We went, not to see her especially, but for blackberries and bluebells. The latter filled us with a kind of lust and were raped, rather than picked, in their hundreds, and for no good reason. Strapped to our bicycles, many of them fell along the road home. It was their delicious heady scent which we carried with us, whilst the long green stalks running to cold ivory slipped from the carrier.

Now, many years and many careers later, Dr.Grace's children, myself and our friends return to Tiger Hill for our yearly reunion called the Bluebell Party, when we picnic in the azure wood and never pick a single flower.

Childhood is, among much else, a matter of attainable destinations. That first getting about on one's own two feet, or one's own two wheels, is a thrilling business. Woods were intensely desirable objectives, High Wood, Acton Wood, Brundon Wood, each beckoned us into its heart and outlawed us. Some were flowerless, all we assumed were ownerless, which was a mistake. Men would appear from nowhere and demand our business and then crash away through the undergrowth. We would continue into the interior, disturbed by the now sensuous smell of leaf-mould and the clatter of frightened birds. We would come to kingdom-like glades or to a solitary figure pollarding. According to stories, woods were where the action was, or from where one might not return, and my heart used to race and thump when I reached them. Always, always I forgot their silence which was in effect the amalgamated sound of their murmuring as the wind fled through them and the movement of animals. When one comes to think about it the sole purpose of a wood in children's literature is to provide a place to get lost in or a place to find freedom in. Looking back, our difficulty must have been to find an unoccupied stretch or two, for 'wooding' was a seasonal activity which brought us to the bluebells, birds' nests and blackberries in chattering packs. Nor had they at that time entirely ceased to be universal providers for the village, and so again seasonally they would be raided for nuts, sloes, bullaces, logs, holly, mistletoe, but never for edible fungi. There were those who viewed the most obvious mushroom with deadly suspicion. Courting was more likely to be confined to the tall meadows and cornfields. Woods made girls uneasy and boys brave. As one grew up, 'going bluebelling' would raise a sexy laugh.

To actually buy a wood, to own and be in possession of one, as is my old friend Richard Mabey, must be among this world's most blissful achievements. Dr. Grace first rented and then purchased Tiger Hill. Her brick cottage with its hut still stand in their little clearing. Whilst Arger Fen itself is managed for today's naturalists and for Sunday afternoon beauty-spot motorists, Tiger Hill is exactly as it was when the first doctors of the Women's Movement created their Lutyenesque hospital for the last of the consumptives on the nearby heights, except that Dr. Grace's children have stealthily added to it pastures, a steep field and one of those half-hidden mile's of grass and shrub always known as the Long Acre, no matter how many scores it might be. There are Arthur Rackham oaks, giant maytrees and wild cherries, the kind which Evelyn called 'mazzards'. There is, too, and unlike most woods, a powerful sense of long human habitation, the actual tree-enclosed homesteads apart. Signs of brickmaking, of timber felling, warrening, basket-weaving, rough farming, and signs of a community which had for generations been cut off by trees and shade from the community proper. Thomas Hardy was born and raised in exactly such a place.

They don't manage the woodland better at Tiger Hill than at Arger Fen, but they manage it differently. The elm skeletons, for instance, stand until they fall, being too many to clear, and have become an accepted part or grade of an ecology which at Tiger

Hill candidly proclaims itself in everything from that old, hidden and enchanting birdsong, to dead trees and mulch, and where the draining, lopping pursuits of poor men have left their scars. Among my first 'friends for life', as Hazlitt described his early companions, was the Cambridge botanist S. D. Garrett and his family. Denis Garrett was the cousin of Millicent Fawcett and Elizabeth Garrett Anderson and, like me, his wife Jane had known Dr. Grace since childhood. I think he was the most single-mindedly absorbed person I have ever met. To remain so, he appeared to have developed a special kind of courtesy which allowed him to descend from what was for me a brilliant specialist science which was so far out of my range that it was futile to imagine that anything I said in this respect could be of the slightest interest to him, and to enter into the general conversation. Yet, out of bounds to my intelligence though his writings on mycology were, the prose itself – like his voice – had a cadence which removed them from the textbook authority to a mysterious kind of art. I found myself reading Denis rather in the way I read Sir Thomas Browne. I tried once to show him how his books appeared in my ignorant eyes by turning a fragment from one of them into a poem. We were sitting in his Cambridge house, Denis working at a card-table in the corner of the room, the Hills Road traffic roaring by, the car, driven by Jane, waiting to take us on an outing to Wicken Fen or some other botanizing jaunt, and myself breaking down (or up) his words on survival into a poem, to his tolerant amusement. It was long ago yet, scientifically or not, this Garrett textbook page into poem goes on connecting me with the funeral of a school-friend, with the white ill Suffolk farm men in their snowy prams, with bony, tanned Dr Grace and with Tiger Hill and its gaunt and shameless dead elms.

Saprophytic Survival

The massive woody root systems
And collar regions of tree species
Differ so much
From the tissues of herbaceous plants
As to make
The problem of saprophytic survival
Quite different in most respects.

The much greater size of tree stumps
And roots,
As well as their mechanical construction,
Greatly reduces
The proportion of extraneous nitrogen
That can diffuse into the inner tissues
From the surrounding soil
- At least during the earlier stages
Of decomposition -
Whilst roots and stumps are still intact.

In the absence of wounds,
The bark offers a mechanical barrier
Of cork tissue
To fungal invasion.
Even after this barrier has been penetrated,
Initial invasion of the wood
Is limited to cellulose – decomposing fungi.
Sylvicultural wounds that expose
Transverse sections of wood,
However,
Will enable non-cellulose decomposers

To invade the lumnia of open vessels.
Another route for more rapid fungal
Invasion
Is provided by the tunnels of beetles.

George Herbert used to say that he felt his consumption was like a mole working away inside him. It is customary to be let down when re-visiting the scenes of youthful excitement, yet not at Tiger Hill or Arger Fen. It could be that they have so much going on in them in the present that they tear one's gaze away from the past. They provide a great display of senescence, but also of nothing going for good. 'Enter these enchanted woods, you who dare,' wrote Meredith in his poem *The Woods of Westermain*. These little woods, about fifty acres in all, were my first sampling of the forest proper. They jut in and out of the corn in such a way that some of the neighbouring fields are like tree-sided rooms with tall green walls. The pastures below the fields have remained as they were and roll into one another in a series of succulent humps, like the meadows in a child's picture-book. Everything rots and thrives.

The Indefinite Shore

It has taken the North Sea just on a thousand years to gnaw away two or three miles of our East Anglian coastline, and these devourings only here and there. Thus we who live by it, one would have thought, would have stepped back a bit when the tides sweep in, and come to some agreement with the floods, rather than fight them. Who ever defeated a sea? The Dutch, we answer. East Anglian fenmen and fishermen-farmers have a lengthy and admiring record of Low Countries' ways. As masters of sea-walls, drains and sluices, it was the Dutch who showed us how to battle it out with waters of all kinds, which meant making the business of keeping the sea out a life's profession for generations of coastal dwellers from the Wash to Canvey Island. The struggle has been heroic, the expense enormous. No one, apparently, proposed an armistice. No one said, 'Let the sea have a nibble and let us stop trying to do the impossible, throwing all our energies into preventing it having a bite of Suffolk, Norfolk and Essex.

Now, after God knows how many generations of flood labour and historic cries of 'Back! Back!', we are to abandon the hopeless task. It is official. The more populated shores will be defended, the less so will give up their ancient resistance and, like a virtuous person who has struggled hard against ravishing, give in to the great wave. It is now almost fifty years since the Great Tide tore in to drown 307 victims and grab 180,000 acres of our property, and loud was the fury about weak defences. But not concrete itself could stem the Great Tide, could cut it into manageable ribbons or delay its arrival. It swept into Holland as well, mocking our heroes, the masters of the dykes, and killing in a single watery night 1,800 Lowlanders, indeed taking vengeance on their sea-defiance and hubris. A near-victim of the deluge in Essex was heard muttering to his rescuers, 'To lie in sleep and awake to drown'. Yet similar flooding must come again, for our coast lists repetitive Great Tides. Spaced out as they are and not racing in every human lifetime. Anyway, they tell us that our Eastern seaboard is a-tilt and that ocean levels are on the rise due to global warming, and building a sea-wall from the Humber to the Thames is out of the question. One day the North Sea will rage through tiny Covehithe roaring 'Remember Dunwich!' for in order to save Aldeburgh such villages must be thrown to it. To us locals it is both shaming and economically sensible that we should rescue the one and not the other. With nearby Dunwich ever in mind – it is Suffolk's watery city of dreams through whose streets the submerged imagination is drawn by strong local currents – the poetry of what is inevitable is permitted, but not the giving in to it. When Wilkie Collins arrived in Aldeburgh in 1862 he began his new novel, *No Name* with what he believed must be obvious to everybody – 'The most striking spectacle by the shores of Suffolk, is the extraordinary defencelessness of the land against the encroachments of the sea', never realising, being a stranger, that the last thing which would strike an East Anglian was his helplessness when it came to a deluge. Which it regularly did. Now the Government's advisers, counting the enormous cost, are telling the North Sea, 'Come in if you must.' Which means saying to the remnants of the ancient prosperity such as tiny Covehithe, 'You may stay undrowned until 2030, or for ever, but that will be up to the sea.' For farmers, landowners and every other kind of native, such an invitation is as outrageous as it is craven.

Covehithe has been going, going, gone by other means than just the sea. As such a victim of trade and water it represents the fate of so many villages and boroughs which once prospered all down the great arc of the East Anglian shore. Yards full of small ships for short journeys, hythes busy with exports, vast churches humming with prayer and pride, some of them like St Andrew's, Covehithe, the most brilliant gull-cages ever made. But this was unintentional and a grief. Those who built it could never have imagined that their descendants would be so broke that they would have to get permission to wreck it and sell the stone. A similar self-ruination occurred at Walberswick twenty years later. The poverty, the cold, the watery miseries, the isolation and desolation of this coast until in recent times it became the sea-side can hardly be described. Best read George Crabbe. Who would retire to his Aldeburgh? Although he fled it, and was to live to see the post-flood squalor of his boyhood gradually give place to some of the elegance of the Regency marine resort, he was always to carry with him a kind of merciless portrait of the type of people which erosion bred. Crabbe is the master of soured land, of the insecure footing, and of a view of society which allows for the sudden descent into either the wilderness of the marshes or the vacuity of the sea. Although a clergyman, the salvation he preached was botany.

One of the curiously depressing aspects of East Anglian coastal erosion is its sordid treatment of plants. Hanks of grass or wheat lie around like heads from the guillotine. Blackthorn and blackberry bushes tangle in ruin with their roots exposed and with evidence of, although they were next-the-sea, little moisture. Cottage gardens are simply shovelled into a big hole, often without a leaf left in sight. The locals always go to look at the latest cliff-fall, boys standing not at all gingerly on the fresh edge, and, should a house have 'gone', everybody wondering as always why there is so little which can be retrieved. It is as though desiccation calls to desiccation with the split, parched quality of each tumble to the beach. Whilst one can meditate on the majesty of the Atlantic overcoming Cornish granite, the manner in which, every now and then, a few tons of East Anglia slips away leaves one with little more than a sense of temporary bewilderment at the havoc, rather than awe at the forces of nature. There is no imperious motion, just slither and crump, dribble and aridity. Should anything like a building or an old road or track be involved, the sight is less archaeologically interesting than just plain miserable. Land-wreckage, like sea-wreckage, drifts, and scraps of one parish sometimes make their way to the next, or become caught in the 'maramels', which is what Lowestoftians used to call their marram dunes. Broken concrete in a cliff-fall presents the most hideous picture of human futility. But broken brick walls are another matter. The sea likes a nice hand-made brick to suck like a sweet and makes a good job of smoothing it away. Where erosion is constant, new surfaces are not given a chance to clothe themselves decently in vegetation and piles of sandy earth, with the promise of plenty more to come, disfigure the coastline. Erosion looks what it is, a mess which can never be cleaned up. Here and there one sees items to provoke thought. Often it is a scattering of graveyard bones, World War II litter, of which there is an enormous amount still, as it was thought that Hitler would invade Britain in 1940 from these easy beaches, and Western Front-like trench soil, which helps to create a suggestion of the shelled landscape of the modern battlefield. And then there are the whole and perfect scenes of sea and land through which the cliff erosion runs like a scar. These offer plenty of balance to what would otherwise be a hopeless perspective. In the famous light which illumines this land one could say that coastal erosion is no more than a nibble. Not more than a mile or two a millennium. It has its good points too. It turns cliffs into beaches. It lets the ocean have a dip into the marches. Has our mistake been to live on top of it, so that we are bound to tumble when the ground gives way under our feet? If so, it is because all along the coast paths from North Norfolk to the Stour estuary there is still so much to remind us of its solid worth.

Most noticeably, there is the grand parade of all-purpose medieval churches with their high seamark towers and enormous naves in which boats might be sold and theatre staged, buildings through which the Reformation flowed on its way to Cambridge. One could make a start with St Margaret's, Cley (pronounced Cly but meaning clay all the same). Here is stone and glass-encased air, with windows set in pairs to divide the full force of the East wind, just as groynes and breakwaters cut through the strength of the sea. Below is the River Glaven and the marshes which are a part of Norfolk's unrivaled kingdom of the birds. Silt fills the harbour where the woolships loaded but a flinty prosperity persists, and those who retire here could get blown away but they are unlikely to share the fate of the coast south of Cromer. Here two villages, Overstrand and Sidestrand, after many years of pre-World War One fame as 'Poppyland', suffered massive cliff-falls. But in the 1880's the theatre critic Clement Scott ('Ibsen's *Ghosts* is a loathsome sore unbandaged') was able to capture all the popular fantasy surrounding drowned churchyards, or in this case a soon to be drowned churchyard, in a poem called *The Garden of Sleep*.

> *In my garden of sleep, where red poppies are spread,*
> *I wait for the living, along with the dead,*

For a tower in ruins stands o'er the deep,

At whose feet are green graves of dear women asleep.

    Did they love, as I love, when they lived by the sea?

    Did they wait, as I wait, for the days that may be?

    Was it hope or fulfilling that entered each breast,

    E'er death gave release, and the poppies gave rest?

      Oh life of my life on the cliffs by the sea!

    By the graves in the grass I am waiting for thee.

        Sleep, Sleep

      In the dews by the deep!

    sleep, my Poppy-land,

      Sleep!

This poem, turned into a drawing-room ballad, swept not only Norfolk but the whole of Britain, and the poppy-crowned heights of that not only eroding farmland but witness to the great agricultural depression, with their narcotic spell, were soon to be linked to the emblematic deathliness of Flanders' fields. As for Clement Scott's church tower, St. Michaels, Sidestrand, built in 1848 to replace the medieval one which had collapsed, it too went over the top, as did the cottage in which Scott had 'immortalised', as they used to say, a local girl. He himself became the almost single-handed promoter of the North Norfolk holiday trade – and the great uncle of Daphne du Maurier. The conquest of the church towers by the sea was to local people something extraordinarily poignant. It was quite a different feeling to that when mud-filled harbours and poverty forced the dismantling and neglect of some of the finest of these relics of a golden age of trade. The parishioners of Sidestrand had taken the main body of their old church down stone by stone, and re-erected it far back from the dangerous edge, where it still stands. But they left the tower – and the dead.

Submerged Dunwich remains, as it has done for centuries, the very capital of erosion. The North Sea began to gulp it down at its most splendid in 1286 and went on devouring it until the tower of the last of its eighteen churches toppled in 1919. A Roman Dunwich floated away before this. The Dunwich which remains is little more than a sandy ledge from which to contemplate what was, what is. Longshoremen squat on it to cast their lines towards streets and squares. Somewhere fathoms deep under the far horizon is the spot where St. Felix strode ashore holding aloft the Gospel for Suffolk. Somewhere below all that water lies a see, a parliamentary division, a city, no less. It invites contemplation. Thomas Girtin, Henry James, Edward Fitz-Gerald, Benjamin Britten, all have paused by the Franciscan gate to allow their fancy free rein. For the coastal dwellers Dunwich has always possessed something akin to the aborigine's dream-line. Romantic marine archaeologists let themselves down into utter blackness to feel for treasure, for a dark veil exists below the surface. Suspended sand and earth particles make it impossible to view the sea-bed. But a few years ago some miraculous current drew it aside and the divers saw St. Peter's Church, lost at sea during the seventeenth century. Most Dunwich searchers have to make do with cornelians and amber, discovered among the pebbles, and plants descended from monastery gardens. Bells, of course, peal beneath the waves.

A few years ago they shifted the huge concrete blocks from where they were laid to halt Hitler, to where they might help to halt the sea. In the past, anything and everything was squashed into a sea-wall, dead sheep, broken ploughs, rotting ships, a fallen tree. The immense shingle ridge running south has always been considered a natural blessing and you could get into serious trouble for taking stones from it. Local records, such as those kept by the Commissioners of Sewers and other bodies, tell of a centuries old determination to keep the sea off the land. There were juries for viewing sea-banks, levels-men, wall-men, marsh-men, bottomfying-men, pumping-plant-men, sea-breach-men, ditching gangs, sluice-cutters, and a muddy army of labourers for defying 'the inroads of the sea'. Generations of coast-dwellers spent their lives doing nothing else. Every river had its own government and the ocean itself its tireless tide-watchers. Where the waters ravaged the dead, their bones would be snatched from the shore and re-buried, some of them over and over again. Now they are left for the waves to gnaw them.

Suddenly, dispassionately, the unequal struggle has been abandoned. A 'National Strategy for Flood and Coastal Defence' advises what it calls 'a managed retreat', carefully like Dunkirk avoiding 'defeat'. A philosopher at the National Rivers Authority was even heard to say, 'It is right to give back land to the sea because we nicked it in the first place.' Words which will make every sluice-cutter squelch in his grave. The National Audit Office washes its hands of the whole liquid business: 'There is no information nationally to access the performance or adequacy of coastal defences.' Meanwhile, the Countryside Commission (the East Anglians can hear the bottomfying-men and their wicked old sea laughing) proclaims, of course, that managed retreat can only enhance its Areas of Outstanding Natural beauty, and that to try to check cliff erosion would not only be an ugly thing to do, but an environmentally damaging thing too. For they would prevent falling soil from renewing the beaches, and divert floods and crumbling earth to other parts. All the same, the budget for such sea and river walls as must remain is enormous – £370 million. Nor can new ways of dealing with the old problem be wholly resisted – what child

can resist trying to dam the runnels of the incoming tide as it
trickles towards his sand-castle? And thus Millennial-men pro-
pose to throw in their lot with levels-men, wall-men, etc. by possibly constructing more off-shore reefs made of concrete similar to those already planned for breaking the sea's strength
between Happisburgh and Winterton. Limited triumphs are
now accepted. Ordinary pine piles from the gloomy Forestry
Commission woods are proving effective in preventing the
banks of the Orwell estuary sliding away. Sploshing around, no
more salutary image than one's early sand-castle can be found.
How ever often it went under, did we not build another? Putting
money and sweat to one side, is there not something compul-
sively satisfying in holding back the ocean, if only for a lifetime, if only for a yard or two?

'Going to the edge' – this was how we inlanders used to think
of a journey to the coast. Its soaring, confident semi-circle on
the map gave East Anglia what looked like a good sound
cranium. Even when evidence to the contrary piled up during
walks in bitter gales, or in surprisingly burning heat, to prove
that our edge wasn't sound at all. Breached by the North Sea by
the day, such softly eroding cliffs were inclined to convey
romance rather than anxiety. The manner in which over the
years houses, towers – everything – ultimately fell off the edge
had long been part of our philosophisings regarding transience
and human endeavour, a notion which gained in piquancy when
a churchyard full of longshoremen and their families dribbled
into the waves. Although threatened communities moved back
a few yards from this land-hungry sea, there had never been an
actual abandonment of the edge – and for obvious reasons. It
was, as well as destructive, an eternal provider. It gave so much
that those who lived on it allowed for its grabbing and taking

appetites. Not that there was any way of stopping them, just as there was no way of diminishing the fish. What the edge had done throughout its human occupation was to acknowledge a tendency to crumble but never that it must become a desolation. Nor even where it petered out in the Wash marshes and failed to draw a line between land and water, had there ever been a giving up of territory to the birds.

But now unprecedented underminings of our watery stoicism have changed all this. The first had nothing to do with coastal erosion and everything to do with the disappearance of the herring. Just imagine if some snatch-all method of arable farming had brought the timeless cycle of the corn harvests to a stop – this is the only way in which the previously unthinkable halting of the North Seas 'silver harvest' of herring can be felt with all of its traumatic force. And not only along our edge but from Scotland to Cornwall.

I am wandering through the paralysed ports of Norfolk and Suffolk during early blustery autumn. The time when the shoals would appear with the certainty of the season itself. There then being no way of catching more than millions, millions more swam on to multiplicity. Then came the hideous international efficiency which landed the lot, the close-mesh trawling, the suction pipes and the purseseine nets which scraped and hoovered up every mite of this swimming harvest, leaving our sea like an aborted womb. Seated in Henry 'Shrimp' Davies's hut on Cromer sands the two of us worry away at this calamity. 'Shrimp' because of the tiny fisher-boy that he was. He shakes his old head at the black miracle which is the obliteration of a fish which only a few years ago was believed to be only a fractionally less numerous than the grains of sand themselves. It is packing-up time on the front when the holiday-making ceases and the town's own leisure begins. Whether end of season or out of season it is hard to find words which adequately describe tides, winds, shutters and stacked chairs. The latter are all Shrimp's. He is Cromer's chair king. Closed down too as any winter pier are the great herring fisheries from Arbroath to St. Ives.

Shrimp meditates. 'You can't believe the industry out there was in the herring trade! A thousand boats out of Yarmouth, a thousand out of Lowestoft. And all the back-up folk – all gone, all gone. And this because of the bloody over-fishing, and scarce one to breed and come by again! You've heard of seed-corn, perhaps? Coming from where you do you would. Well, think about it. Think about thoughtlessness – or sheer bloody greed more like! They did it to the mackerel, they did it to the sprats, and they'll do it to every living thing – you'll see! Yes, once thousands and thousands of us fishing and making boats and boxes and baskets, and the harbours a forest of masts, and the herring coming by for ever.'

A single steam-drifter provided a living for upward a hundred workers, they said. Now, should the herrings be tempted or nursed back in their old multitude? Will we eat them as we once did, or will our pets? A folk-connection between this particular sea-food and hard times tends to dismiss their deliciousness and put them rather low on the shopping-list – though never on mine, where they remain a treat. Long ago, making do in a little house on the shingle, writing stories and poems, and practising acute economies, I would crunch along the stones in the early morning and buy a shilling's worth from a boat, and receive as many as two hands could manage, slippery and iridescent breakfasts for the week. *Clupea harengus* whose bone-pattern inspired our brick-work. Will the ancient Fish-churches straddling the edge of East Anglia be the last things to declare the herring's greatness – just as the Wool-churches of the interior go on telling us that sheep once made millionaires too? Let us also remember those Great Yarmouth benefactors, Mr. Bishop the inventor of the bloater and Mr. Woodger the creator of the kipper. Humble glories.

Shrimp, like every old fisherman-cum-lifeboatman, is a mixture of free talk and impenetrable reserve. He is poised, playful and unhurried, having ascended the throne of one of the country's best known coastal families. From the time they emigrated from Wales in the 1820's, the Davieses, Cromer's crab fishery and the town's celebrated lifeboat history have been all one. Since 1872 to the present the family has doubled as local fishermen with an oar, so to speak, in the holiday trade, and as heroes. Had there been a time when Shrimp had fancied another sea? His light-ruined eyes look back on an ad about adventurous boys setting out to fish tuna off Australia. And he would have gone with other Cromer lads, except for that shout from his father. 'Oh no you won't! You'll stay here where you bloody belong!' And he'd stayed, to become coxswain of the *Henry Blogg* lifeboat in 1948 and the inheritor of deckchairs and beach huts. He said that the young no longer hire either. Just strip off on the sand. It was his grandfather, lifeboat coxswain during the 1890's, who had invested in the great cumbrous bathing machines from which Shrimp's daringly flimsy box-tents had descended. These were actually a Davies invention and their blenched colours set against the clarity of the East Beach with its striped bodies caught the palette of Wilson Steer. It struck me that Shrimp and the discreet bathing business were not unhappy to be seeing each other out. The trade had made him an expert in packing-up. He ran a huge hand over a sagging chair. 'Mind you, their frames must be as old as mine!' Like everything else, like muttering, 'In the name of the Lord' every time you cast your net, modern indifference to ritual tends to thin both the splendours and the absurdities of life.

A splendour. 'The Empress Elizabeth of Austria was a sick lady who came to Cromer for the air, you know. They all did then. She changed in grandfather's big old horse-drawn machine and when she came out, there he'd be, trim in his snow-white ducks and marking a special spot for her Majesty to swim around. To keep her safe, you know.'

For the Davies family the shoreline is written all over with myriad fantasies and mundane ventures which the sea muddles. One day it is harvesting crabs from the rocks, the next souls from the wrecks, both activities becoming somehow natural concomitants of each other. And so it has been with all the hereditary masters of this capricious circumflex of ocean as it gnaws its way into the Gaps. The Gaps are where, from Lincolnshire to Essex, the North Sea thrusts in. At Cromer the lifeboat lives just behind the Pavilion Theatre, and the thought that the stage curtains and the sea doors are only a few yards away from each other is both exciting and sobering. Small boys stare through knotholes at the churning tide. Davies boys had their first trip in the lifeboat long before they were seventeen – the permitted age. And all were seasick. Being seasick is thought neither a weakness nor a matter of other people's comment by fishermen and sailors. When you grew up you learnt how to be totally sick at the beginning of a run but not to feel ill afterwards. It was an art. 'Once I was cox'n I was never seasick,' grinned Shrimp, trusting that I was getting the drift of this. Like the current lifeboat, the *Ruby and Arthur Reed II*, he doubles as a holiday attraction and a challenger of the North Sea's claim to gorge on men and ships at will. He shares with Cromer a dated, bastioned, don't-think-you-will-ever-wash-me-away quality.

Frenchified once-posh hotels straddle the cliff-top and just beyond them can be seen the grand medieval church. The town has got off lightly where the developers are concerned and hasn't had its heart torn out to make space for shopping malls. It retains its hugger-mugger lanes and courts, its flinty walls and orange pantiles, and hasn't given way to very much since its florid Edwardian summer. But nobody stays in a hotel or a boarding-house for a week any more, nobody parades along the parade. The nice train from Norwich decants just me and a couple of others, and not the seasonal multitude. It is the car and the tour bus, the one-night stayers who eat their way round Britain. A whole *week* in Cromer? Why not? It could amaze you. But it could be too melancholy, like a street when the band has gone by, although I don't find it so. I find myself tapping into the old resourcefulness and searching for jet, amber and chalcedony along the beach, and sea-lavender, buckthorn, purslane, centaury, vetches and glasswort on the headlands, which blow your head off. I would be thinking about murder or love and the gulls would howl.

Fishermen-lifeboatmen never for one moment take their eyes off what is happening here. It is Richard Davies, Shrimp's nephew, who is now principal watcher in these long linked occupations. He is forty-two and has already been lifeboat cox'n for a decade. 'I was the youngest cox'n in the country when I took over from Shrimp and I'll stay cox'n until I'm fifty-five.' Shrimp, as everybody knows, had the daunting task of having to take over from the immortal Henry Blogg, the R.N.L.I.'s greatest hero, the taciturn little man who served in Cromer's lifeboats for 53 years, during which time he saved 873 lives. Mild yet awesome, Blogg's brilliant seamanship accompanied a kind of constant fearlessness. What to most men is a rush of courage to deal with a crisis was for Blogg his normal state of mind. The illegitimate child of a girl who married into the

Davies family, he has become the Titan who towers over it, giving it unchallengeable identity. He gave Shrimp both his Christian and nickname. 'What a bloody shrimp!' brave uncle Henry had said, looking at the new baby. Nicknames were once as necessary as proper names on this coast. A roll-call is like an extension to Shakespeare's mechanicals. Squinter, Snouts, Teapot, Pokey, Tweet – and Posh, of course. It seems shocking to fix them to the grave and noble faces on the old photographs. Nearly all the fishermen-lifeboatmen were Nonconformists and their sobriquets, from which there was no escape, are debased versions of the old Puritan nomenclature of East Anglia. 'A nickname is the heaviest stone that the devil can throw at a man', Hazlitt said – a verdict which would have puzzled Yarmouth 'Rednecks', Lowestoft 'Pea-bellies' and the 'Joskins' who were half fishermen-lifeboatmen and half farm labourers. The robustness of these old days still clings to Shrimp, but so too does a different kind of language, that which is learnt from reading very little, but this of the best.

Joseph Conrad was taught his first English lessons by men like the Davieses when he worked aboard the Lowestoft collier *Skimmer of the Sea*, and he liked to say that the North Sea was 'the schoolroom of my trade'. When Shrimp was a lad he read a poem about Cromer which he has been trying to find ever since. At last somebody has sent it to him. It is by Jean Ingelow and is much longer and entirely different to what he imagined. Shrimp had been waiting a lifetime for a ballad about a Cromer girl keeping vigil 'on the green downs' for a fisherman who will never return. Drowned. Now it appears that she is grieving for a boy who fell off a mountain. 'There's *The High Tide on the Coast of Lincolnshire*', I suggest, turning it up. But he wants the poem which was never written. Above him 'on the green downs' the

62

bronze sou-westered bust of Uncle Henry Blogg, George Cross, with its long nose and gentle expression, stares down on the crab boats and the crotchety tractors which drag them over the shingle, Cox'n Blogg who neither smoked nor drank, but who knew how to be caustically witty in the local manner when he had a mind to.

Young Davieses have a way of guarding tradition without being old-fashioned. All the same, they are aware, though not self-consciously so, that history, occupation and duty have isolated them from what most people experience. They maintain distinctions of dress – always a jersey under a jacket for a wedding – and of speech. Richard Davies, putting down the crabpot he is mending; 'Now I wouldn't say the 'last' pot – always the 'finishing one'. We never say last. And I'd never start a season on a Friday if there were a thousand crabs! Wouldn't move house on a Friday neither. Due to it being Crucifixion day, perhaps? When the alarm goes in the night Julie's job is to unlock the door for me to run through. She waits here and never runs with me to watch, though some do. You run from wherever you are – you run! I've tied the dog to a lamp-post – and run! Our gear is in the boat and we put it over what we are wearing, and on the way we discuss what we should do. Sometimes we sail far, once nearer to Holland than to Norfolk. Its bad when you find people who have brought tragedy on themselves. And you have to be tactful with idiots, who are very frightened. Fortunately, we don't get a silly season like those sailing places. Ours is mostly commercial shipping. Things for us are never as safe as they look, There's still more than one lifeboat lost a year and how many crew, I don't know. We officially practise every six weeks but as we are fishermen we practise every day of our lives. The main danger would be turning over, our new boat is a self-righter, but when I started they were open boats. So there you were, out in the cockpit all the time. Our boat the *Ruby and Arthur Reed II* is one of the most sophisticated in the fleet. We always call her 'our' boat. The strongest things which you see on land which you see from the sea are church towers, although not Cromer tower. It hides. We are inbred to these tasks, to this life. They say the first lifeboatmen were the hovellers. When there was a wreck the best hoveller oarsmen would get there first and so they would get the goods. And the not so fast hovellers would get there second, and they got the crew! That's how we started, they say. They said the North Norfolk fishermen could row best and the Yarmouth fishermen could sail best. They'd race the lifeboats, and we'd have to row ours to the race first. Thirty mile. I'd say before my time!'

No one could ever have imagined that the mighty herring fleets would be annihilated and that the little crabbers would not only survive but flourish. Although the Cromer crab-boats have shrunk from fifty to fifteen, seven of which are owned by the Davieses, their catch is still in great demand. It was the Davieses' foresightedness which preserved the crabs on their rocky ledge, and it was they and their neighbours who got Parliament to make a law which forbade the taking of crabs which were less than four and half inches across, and lobsters under eight inches. These crab-fishing grounds are about three miles off-shore and stretch from Cley to Mundesley, and they are fished from April to September by two men and some two hundred crab-pots per boat. The pots hang together in strings or 'shanks', with an anchor and a buoy at each end. On a good day, or rather a good night, a boat can return to Cromer with a catch of eight hundred crabs. The crab-pots are baited with nice fresh fish, usually from Lowestoft, and are emptied just before daybreak. Lobsters prefer bait which is a bit more stinko. During the winter months crabbers will get a kind of catch-crop by sailing to Palling to set pots for whelks.

Richard Davies makes his own pots in the yard behind his fish shop in Garden Street. His strong hands fly through the scarlet mesh. The pots are very elegant and look as though they would double as bird cages. Each has a massive gridded bottom to steady it against the currents. In Richard and Julie's home between the net-yards and the fish-shop sepia faces from the past fill the picture-frames, as do stiff paintings of heavy wooden boats on fierce seas. Every lifeboatman-fisherman's house in Sheringham, Sidestrand, Caister, Overstrand, Yarmouth and Lowestoft contains a similar brave gallery. The photographs are the kind to which the viewer himself has to add colour. I add azure streaking into dank slate, oyster rifts in the sky, blue to eyes, red-brown to skin.

'Talking of eyes,' says Richard, 'I don't think much of the R.N.L.I. at this moment. It is all this fuss they are making about being colour-blind. Good lifeboatmen are having to go because they are colour-blind. Two stations from here, Wells to be exact, they've lost their second cox'n, the best man they have and the skipper of his own fishing boat, and why? Because they found out he was colour blind! And I had two young boys who were as good as any crew members in England, but now no more! Colour-blind. Supposing Henry Blogg had been tested and found colour-blind – then what? I think the Institution should leave the picking of crews to men like us – I do straight! Men may be bad on reds and greens, but what of that?'

Early the following morning I watched Shrimp rolling towards the East Beach, the only person in sight, his face 'coloured like a postcard' as Joseph Conrad described his shipmates, the North sea flashing in his big spectacles and his navy jersey rucked across his fat belly. Choppy waves ran to meet him.

The Shepherd Observed

The vicarage children have descended from exploring the roof-space with armloads of old newspapers. 'There are hundreds – thousands – of them'. Don't exaggerate. They turn out to be a Victorian insulation against the draughts. The boys dump them on the carpet in clouds of dust. There is a smell of another day. They are almost exactly one hundred years old, *The Times, The Church Times* and *The Ecclesiastical Gazette.* Ancient Anglican news crumbles from them and into our nostrils. We sit on the floor and read out the juicy bits. Fearful assizes, angry deans; Mr. Stanley is 'gradually emerging from the black depths of the dark continent' after his efforts 'to rescue one who, it seems, was not quite sure whether he wanted to be rescued or not'. 'General' Booth is being tiresome about money, needing lots of it. He needs to be watched. Magic lanterns are £7.17s and fares to Sydney on the Orient line £17.17s. The 'largest and loveliest cemetery in the world' is near Woking. The letters page is fretful. 'Sir, can any of your readers tell me if any legal means exist of stopping irregular marriages?' Villagers are getting wed in town churches, rather than in their own parish church, in order to find some privacy in their lives. There is advice on how to recruit farm-labourers for the army. Nearly three thousand acres of first class farmland near Beccles are to be let for shooting. Polite journalism is no more than a veneer for the rough news, the rough voices, the rough prospects.

Grandmother, it occurred to me, would herself have been getting married when Mr. Hargraves' back'us boy heaved all this newsprint into the loft and spread it between the joints, and on her way to Cuckoo Tye. Not that she would have seen this vicarage because it was all of thirty miles from home, although the same winds howled through it. Her 'Tye' would be on the high ground equidistant from Long Melford and Lavenham, both of whose church towers would stand as markers in the landscape for the rest of her life. These tyes were a feature of our part of Suffolk. They were little communities which had grown up around either a remote farm or a common pasture far from the main village, although hers had been gathered-in by Earl Howe, whose coronet marked one of the main buildings. But generally, like Thomas Hardy's woodlanders and heath-landers, the folk spent centuries out of sight. It did not make them especially independent, simply isolated. Cuckoo Tye itself was – is – a small moated farm at the end of a wide green land. The once common pasture close by was a hamlet named Newman's Green, a place full of relations once or twice removed, so that we never did quite know the connection. It was the heyday of honorary aunts and uncles, rather as all cooks were called Mrs. Concealing bastardy became an art-form, the truth only coming out when some liaison threatened to come uncomfortably near the list of whom one may not marry which hung in the church porch. The list was so long that most rural populations would have died out had it been obeyed to the letter. However, obedience has never been East Anglia's strong point.

Paths from the Tye were grassy and fugitive, and much ploughed over now. They tended to skirt the main village but make bee-lines for the neighbouring town, as though those travelling them longed occasionally to be swallowed up. Grandfather, taking Suffolks to Norfolk, would have by-passed Acton, his native village, but most likely have driven his sheep through

Lavenham, Bury St. Edmunds and all metropolises to Dereham, simply to see the sights, though staying hidden on the way. He died when I was six and remains a quizzical authoritarian whose sky-blue eyes and brown face under a weathered hat created uncertainty. He petted and mussed children much as he did sheep-dogs or, similarly, bade them to be quiet and sit. 'Do what he says,' advised Grandmother. Their house, although never free of people coming and going, was at heart impressively still, a place where clocks were encouraged to have their own voice. After Grandfather's death she married an aged widower, once a schoolfriend who had missed her the first time round, and the quietness of the house continued to defeat the noise of talk and feet. She lived long enough to glimpse our first television set, a sturdy affair with the lines of a fruit machine. 'I have to ask a question: can *they* see *us*?' In the quiet house she and her second husband used their wireless for the Service. Born in 1860 – years before Thomas Hardy had written a word – they were thankful for such modern convenience as being able to have the Service without having to go to church.

Whilst she was alive I found myself less fascinated by Grandmother's ancient farming roots than by her longevity. Dwelling on it eventually produced a non-gerontological defence of old age. My researches, some of them at least, were to be as fugitive as the boy shepherd David Blythe's travels with his flock. And thus I entered the centre of Lavenham to meet Major Bush né Michael Home, who was ninety and lived at the Great House. Major Bush, as Michael Home, had written a dozen books about his childhood in the Breckland in what could be construed as an attempt to reconcile his early self with the person he became after success as a writer of Thirties' whodunnits, and what he called 'novels of military intelligence'. He was born in 1885 and had been a prolific author, his village tales full of fierce loyalty to Hockham, the place where mallows grew. The Breckland was East Anglia's heath, not an Egdon with furzy arms upraised to dash human hopes, but an airy desert where rabbits and foxes excavated the flint axes and chisels left behind by neolithic walkers. It was all farmed and afforested out of existence after the First World War. Major Bush as Michael Home gave scrupulous chapter and verse on the life led there, the rabbits grown to a great plague, the bracken closing-in the paths, the gamekeepers rubbing their hands, the farmers perishing. But sitting by an old man's cindery gate in the kitchen of the Great House, we did not talk of such things, or of shepherd David brazenly running his sheep across the market square outside, or of anything literary. I saw the little Breckland cottage and the Great House, the shuffle through the fine rooms to the warm, sweet-smelling kitchen and the wooden armchair. And I saw, as in many an ancient man, a recidivist. Outside, Lavenham's late-medieval glories were in the restorative hands of a new race, the retired, with its understanding and appreciation of such things. Taking stock of these beam-worshippers, the postman observed, 'They say Lavenham is God's waiting-room'. It is quite something to have lived long enough to have known a man who drove sheep through a Suffolk wool-town now filled with Japanese photographers, and no lament is intended. It is just the phenomenon, the outlandishness, which cannot be avoided. As boys, my brothers and I would climb the church tower, the mightiest in the county, and look down on the ploughing and the entire world of what in the fifteenth century was a millionaire's manufactuary. The scene was concise, the church excepting, a town of wood in High Suffolk, with orange tiles and its fairytale roofs abundant with stonecrop and house-leeks, the latter to keep the witches away. And to the south, far off, the magenta rise of the Essex hills. Below lay Shilling Street, Water Street, Lady Street and Prentice Street. The masterly church itself appeared to us to have tree-like origins, for it was the creation of men named Spring and Branch, and of Lord Oxford, whose badge was a boar. The churchyard was full of gypsies, whose vardoes wintered on the heath. Grandmother remembered seeing one burnt after a death. There would have been gypsies on the Breckland when Major Bush was Michael Home. One of the legendary travelling women was Ocean, whose territory stretched to south Norfolk. Moving about so much herself, would Ocean have noticed 'the flight from the land'?

This is what they called it, anxiously, in the late-Victorian newspapers. The labourers, the servants, they were taking wing. Henry Rider Haggard, the farmer who wrote novels, prefaced his *Rural England* – 'being an account of agricultural and social researches carried out in the years 1901 & 1902' – with a quotation from the Book of Judges. 'The highways were unoccupied...the inhabitants of the villages ceased.' Lavenham was half empty between the wars and the poor who lived in the huge timbered loom-rooms shivered in winter, and papered the beams to make some cosiness. Some biked seven miles to Sudbury to make silk for, among other things, Queen Mary's parasols and frontals for cathedrals. Also old school ties and corsets. They cycled in groups singing songs. There was a lot of movement as if to balance so much stillness. It was penury time and if you weren't on the go you could hear a pin drop. Keeping on the go was the thing.

Collecting information for his book on 'the flight from the land', Rider Haggard arrived in Grandfather's home ground. The novelist was in his mid-forties when he took stock of this countryside, much the same age as David the shepherd of Cuckoo Tye, whose only flight was the swift return from the depressed markets. Haggard himself farmed 365 acres of beautiful land where the Bath Hills and the Waveney Valley opened towards Bungay. Two years before he had made a brave effort to put the heart back into East Anglian agriculture by writing a candid diary called *A Farmer's Year*, in which nothing was held back and the profit and loss, chiefly the latter, was set out to the last penny. This bitter-sweet journal of what was happening on his own farms – then two of them, one in Ditchingham, the other in Bedingham – was suggested by Tusser's *Hundreth Good Points of Husbandrie*, a rhymed farm book written by a professional musician in 1557. The scene was Tusser's riverside farm, at Cattiwade, the scene which John Constable would paint when, yet again, British agriculture had collapsed. Tusser was wry.

> *Who minds to quote*
> *Upon this note*
> * May easily find enough:*
> *What charge and pain,*
> * To little gain*
> * Doth follow toiling plough.*

Haggard was hopeful. The prosperity would come back if only the labourers would cease to fly away. Why flee to the towns? 'What kind of places are these cities to live in, for the poor?' What kind of places were Ditchingham and Bedingham – and Acton – for that matter, for fieldworkers on ten bob a week? Or indeed for near-bankrupt farmers? A few months before writing his honest, pleading journal, (come back, Hodge, all is forgiven for it acknowledged the men's wonderful skills),

Haggard had visited Egypt and seen the paintings and reliefs on the royal tombs at Sakkara, and had thought how very like he himself was to the 'gentlemen-farmers of the Fifth and Sixth Dynasties who, whilst yet alive, caused their future sepulchres to be adorned with representations of such scenes of daily life and husbandry as to them were most pleasant and familiar'. Egypt had had its plagues, but they passed, and the joy of the cornfields remained. So stand firm, was his advice to East Anglia, 'although how the crisis will end it is not possible for the wisest among us to guess today'. He could not have guessed that the crisis would not end until 1940, when Hitler's war inaugurated the second agricultural revolution and today's corn and dairy surpluses.

Haggard was a celebrity when he came to Grandfather's patch. Not only had he written *A Farmer's Year*, 'my commonplace book for 1898', but *King Solomon's Mines, She,* and *Allan Quatermain.* These colourful African bestsellers stemmed from his other life. At nineteen he too had fled the family acres in Norfolk for opportunities in South Africa, where he joined the staff of Sir Theophilus Shepstone and had with his own hands raised the Union flag in Pretoria's main square. Revered by the Africans, detested by the Boers, Shepstone had annexed the Transvaal for Queen Victoria almost single-handed, and without consulting her government. The resulting turmoil finished his career. Shepstone's unorthodoxy and dash enthralled the youthful Haggard and fed his imagination. When he returned to Norfolk, still only twenty-four, he became a very unusual member of the county's farming, sporting gentry. These too, as much as the labourers, he saw, were stuck in some kind of inertia and fatalism. Why could not both be like those glorious tillers of the soil on the tombs at Sakkara? What had happened to make English farmwork so despised, so appalling? He visited Heckingham Workhouse.

'What do these old fellows think about, I wonder, as they hobble to and fro round those measureless precincts of bald brick? The sweet-eyed children that they begot and bred-up fifty years ago, perhaps? Whose pet names they still remember, now dead or lost to them for the most part; or the bright waving cornfields whence they scared birds when they were lads from whom death and trouble were yet a long way off. I dare say, too, that deeper problems worry them at times in some dim half-apprehended fashion; at least I thought so when the other day I sat behind two of them in a church near the workhouse. They could not read, and I doubt if they understood much of what was passing, but I observed consideration in their eyes. Of what? Of the terror and the marvel of existence, perhaps, and of that good God whereof the person is talking in those long unmeaning words. God! They know more of the devil and all his works; ill-paid labour, poverty, pain, and the infinite unrecorded tragedies of humble lives. God? They never found Him. He must live beyond the workhouse wall – out there in the graveyard – in the waterlogged holes which very shortly . . .'

In all Haggard employs some fifteen men on his farms. Their dogged strength amazes him, isolates him from them. In January he had watched a pair of them bush-draining a huge expanse of clay land. It had taken them ten weeks and at the end 'such toilers betray not the least delight in the termination of their long labour'. It was just the same with dyke-drawing, the toughest of all winter jobs. They dug a twelve-hour day in summer and when ever it was light in winter, and without holidays. And yet, something 'teaches them that there are places in the world besides their own village' and makes them aspiring and restless. More and more of them disappear, making for the army, the colonies, the Lowestoft fishing smacks, anywhere preferable to a Norfolk farm. It grieves him. Their lives are dreadful, but they should not be. He should be like them, a Boaz gathering in the harvest beside them, but he cannot be. Sir Theophilus was nearer to his Africans than Squire Haggard to his ploughmen. Unwittingly, *A Farmer's Year* captures the sullenness of the flying away and the coming-down time.

Rider Haggard's report from Grandfather's world was severe. Ruined cottages at 1s. 6d. a week. Labour at thirty shillings the acre. The farmer saying, 'the better you farmed the less you made'.

'Within two miles of Lavenham the country was bleak, lonesome, and undulating. Here we saw some empty cottages, also winter barley, which is grown to a certain extent in this district. The cottages were very bad and had leaky roofs. My companions informed me that, taking the average of these parishes, they were badly farmed and full of misery. Indeed they all declared that 'the industry is in a parlous state – on the verge of ruin, in fact.'

Wages were 10s. for old men but up to 20s. for engine-drivers and stockmen. Horses were cheaper than steam ploughs. Farms were being sold for £7 10s. the acre. There were masses of poultry and few sheep. The pastures were going back, the arable land becoming wilds. A Clare farmer told Haggard that 'for the eight years that he had lived there he had been trying to get on better terms with his men, but was as far as ever from this consummation. The feeling between employers and employed was bad, and to get a job done he must stand over his labourers, and nothing but actual poverty would drive a man to hard toil. He was sick of Suffolk men and, if he could house them, he would bring down men from the Shires, even if he had to pay them £1 a week.' The Rector of Earl Soham deplored the badness of the Suffolk roads. 'The primary cause of this, I believe, is the doing away with the system of picking stones in the fields, due to the advance of education'. Rider Haggard said he had been thrown off his bicycle when riding along equally atrocious roads nearer home. At Acton and its Tye the farmers were 'rubbing along'. The men there 'took no interest in their tasks', he was told. All the young fellows had gone fifteen years later when Rider Haggard passed by, longing to ennoble the disenchanted scene, aching to make it like the fields of Sakkara, where the husbandry was touched by divinity. Instead, Lord Howe's agent told him that things were as bad as they well could be, and that there was no hope for the future of Suffolk agriculture. But when, as a boy, I sat with the ancient relations and honorary relations in their apple-scented houses, I cannot remember them being marked by despair. Physically, even when thin, they had a monolithic quality, a presence not unlike the reapers and herdsmen at Sakkara. They were cagey about their lot, or perhaps unable to put it into words. Due to the camera, they were the first generation of farming folk to possess a portrait gallery. There they hung, two or more generations of the family, the photographs blown up until they were a mass of pointillistic dots, and heavily framed, among them the departed. Not only the dead but the fled.

Whilst Rider Haggard was writing *King Solomon's Mines* at Ditchingham a young American doctor arrived in East Anglia to photograph the 'peasants'. The name P. H. Emerson drifts around in the local consciousness in a still quite powerful way, and there might still be cottages with an Emerson on the walls, for he was kind to his sitters, or usually toilers. His masterpieces had titles like 'Coming Home from the Marshes', 'Women Raking', the marvellous 'Gathering Waterlilies', which is a Monet done with a lens, and 'Yarmouth from Breydon Water'. He has been seen as the first photographer-poet to arrive on a frenetic scene in which men with cameras were striving to make much the same reputations as men with palettes and engraving tools. Dr. Pedro Enrique Emerson was twenty-seven when he first saw East Anglia and instantly recognised it as the ideal region for providing him with the material for his big statement, which was that photography was better than painting and sculpture. Superior. A great step forward. Fair, tall, freshly wed, a cousin of Ralph Waldo Emerson, possessing dual English and New England nationality, he might have come straight out of a Henry James novel. Before coming to Southwold, he had been to Rome, where the pictures and statues shocked the Puritan, agnostic and anatomist in him. Somebody gave him a camera and with it he intended to give the lie to Art. The intensification of the natural view, via the lens, was to remain for him the camera's ultimate glory. He agreed with his Suffolk and Norfolk 'peasants' when he permitted them to put their heads beneath his focusing cloth, and when they caught their breath with delight at a brilliance which they had never before seen, and said, 'Ah, if we could only get it like that!' Life, they meant. For Emerson and for his subjects revelation came through ground glass.

Emerson had a few lessons, not from a photographer, but from his old tutor in physics and chemistry at Cambridge. He was one of those artists who require just a feather-like instruction, as had Julia Margaret Cameron, his heroine. Presented by her daughter and son-in-law with a lens and dark box – 'It may amuse you, Mother, to try to photograph' – she turned her coal cellar into a dark-room, her hen-house into a glass-room, and began to take pictures immediately. When Emerson came to Southwold he at once gave up medicine, engaged the local artist and naturalist, T. F. Goodall, to guide him around the district, and set-to on a series of albums, *Life and Landscape on the Norfolk Broads, Pictures of Life in Field and Fen, Idylls of the Norfolk Broads, Pictures of East Anglian Life* and *Wild Life on a Tidal Water*.

When published these wonderful picture-books were received with every kind of hostility and criticism. Also with some kind of awe. The new photographic establishment, with its journals and medals, and its crusade to place itself as an equal among painters and engravers, saw all that it believed in threatened by what Emerson called his Naturalistic Photography. It was all too natural for photographers like Henry Peach Robinson, who said, 'It is the photographer's duty to avoid the mean, the bare, the ugly, and to correct the unpicturesque.' Emerson, who quite liked a row, attacked this school for years and years. In a way, it assisted him to draw ever closer to his controversial vision, that of the half-marine, half-agricultural society semi-starving on its watery acres.

There was another enemy, the local press, which had no doubt what this grand American doctor was getting at, which was something called 'making trouble'. Its columns were filled with Tory rage by this exposure, in captions, and essays, as well as photographs, of the miserable conditions in which the rural poor lived. Emerson, unlike Peach Robinson and his tribe, who combed the alleys and seafronts for beautiful or striking faces, and bodies which could be dressed up to create genre-pictures, published his portraits of a coastal people in order that his work 'would help in the understanding of this peculiar region and to the outcry against abuses', He recorded the local dialect and learned all the local crafts and customs. And, as a doctor, he noted the local health and welfare. He became, in Nancy Newhall's words, 'a prophet crying in a strange, dry mechanised and mercantile wilderness'. Dry in the Eliot sense. In 1891 Emerson gave it all up. He sent a letter to every photographic magazine saying that 'the medium must rank the lowest of all arts ... In short, I throw my lot in with those that photography is a very limited art. I regret deeply that I have come to this conclusion'. He lived on until 1935, ten years after grandfather, who never came into his view-finder but who would have made a good subject. Especially in the 1880's when he was in his twenties, and journeying on and on with his flock. Emerson immortalised, if photography can do such a thing, his peasants on a grey day 'when possible'. Staring into his view-finder, they saw one another vivid as dragonflies and existing in a jewel. Critics began to talk of Courbet and Millet when they looked at his work. Visiting the Broads cottages and hovels, Emerson gasped at the closeness and the stench.

If Rider Haggard describes the abandonment of the villages, his Norfolk neighbour, Mary Mann, provides us with the most relentlessly truthful account of village existence at its nadir. Her husband farmed 800 acres and from their home, Shropham Manor, she observed without camera and economics exactly what was going on. It was the age of dialect, folksong and folkdance collecting, and her popular country novels were at first vehicles for rustic speech and customs. Then something happened. The caste tragedy of 'condition' suffuses the text and dialect becomes the cry of the trapped. Here are men and women planted as immutably in the Norfolk clay as were their ancestors, and as are the crops. When they talk it is the speech of plight, and Mary Mann puts it all correctly down, offering no assistance, and it is only by stoically enduring their misfortune of birth, their ignorance and their incessant labour that her characters are able to achieve something which her readers can admire. Her terrible understanding of what is happening in the local cottages and in her own land is at its best when it comes to describing the actual nervelessness, apathy and inertia which comes, not so much from being stuck in a rut, as from being tethered from birth on a few sour acres. She states that these villagers inhabit 'an insignificant landscape, black fen-land, gorse-choked heath, familiar ponds and pits and puddles, rank turnip fields, flat distances ...' They inhabit, in fact, all that we now find conservationally desirable.

However, the common dilemma of the Emerson-Haggard-Mann fieldworker is to find 'the Book of Life practically closed'. Against the stark facts of their education, religion, diet, marriage, toil, sickness and death, Mary Mann now and then pulls out some not quite done-for creature from these 'poor units of the brutish, measureless human undergrowth.' Also, and unlike Henry Haggard, she fails to acknowledge the skills of the farms, the wonderful ploughing and reaping and care of the animals. What she does see is an understandable running away from rural depression for those with the strength to do so, and an equally understandable collapse into drink and squalor by those left behind. Shropham, her own parish, which she calls 'Dulditch', is depopulated by a third during her lifetime. The flight feeds her radicalism and she often appears self-surprised by the relentlessness of her own pursuit of the sad stay-at-homes in their muddle of fortitude, eccentricity, vice and penury. She must have worried the Edwardian lady. There is no 'politeness'. The politeness is in the local press which cannot bear to think that if everything on the cottage garden isn't lovely, it will soon be so. Mary Mann, the farmer's wife, thought that the average field-worker's fate was so ghastly that he must be under some special curse from on high. Henry Rider Haggard wanted to stand in the field, a man with his men, but found them more unlike himself than a Zulu. Pedro Enrique Emerson from New England captured them body and soul on a grey day. Mary Mann, infinitely better than any dialect-lorist, has caught their actual voice, thus undermining her sense of their hopelessness, for it comes through witty and strong. There is little wrong with these East Anglians but everything wrong with the social and economic system of the day which sees them simply as 'hands'. Henry Rider Haggard, of course, believed in passing through fire to become immortal. I had no idea when I was twelve that he had composed a fat two-volume inventory of the collapse of agriculture at the turn of the century, and of the flight from it. But I read all about Ayesha and Allan Quatermain, as I lay hidden from 'jobs' in the tall summer grass in the lanes and meadows leading to Cuckoo Tye, and thrilled to the fiery transformation process. Something of this solution runs through his bitter *Rural England*. What other agricultural advisor to the government – he was to be knighted for his farming expertise, and not for his fiction – would preface a study about people like Grandfather with the text, 'I will make a man more precious than fine gold; even a man than the golden wedge of Ophir.' And, with set-aside and golf courses proliferating all around me, it is salutary to read at the close of Haggard's view of Grandfather's world, 'I am sure that one of the worst fates which can befall England is that her land should become either a playground or a waste ...'

Going to meet George

Why, I ask myself, is Canada so near and Orkney so far? This was not only because the customer next to me in the travel office was paying so much less for her fare to Toronto than I was for my fare to Kirkwall. I had explored Orkney on the page but never on the ground, I knew well its seventy green islands which were scattered on the Atlantic in the pattern made by the fleshless bones of the hand, and I knew that the distance to anywhere must always be more than a mileage. In 1967 some stories by George Mackay Brown called *A Calendar of Love* taught me something fresh about distance. He and I would be given consecutively the Society of Authors' Travel Scholarship, and George, already famous for going nowhere, had plucked up courage to blue his on a trip to Ireland, where he stayed with Seamus Heaney. George would be over seventy when our mutual friend Hugo Brunner gave him his first glimpse of London. I had tramped round Skye in my twenties but even when I was that far north Orkney held the remoteness of one of those places which are just off the map in an atlas, and which have to be brought forward in a little box all to themselves at the foot of the section. Entrancing inner guides to Orkney in the guise of George's poetry and tales arrived in Suffolk, and we wrote to each other, though he never added, 'Come and see me should you ever find yourself in Stromness', for how unlikely that would be! We judge friends by our own likelihoods.

But eventually I went. I tore myself from George's geography where sometimes one never knew which century one was in, and bought a ticket to Kirkwall. I thought it best not to tell him and just went. When we met I would say that I had suddenly found myself in his country – Orkney is actually a Scottish county, which sounds odd – and it would be a kind of truth. And he, being considerably visited, as poets who dwell at the ends of the earth often are, would not be all that amazed and would say, 'Come in'. It would be as if I walked along Dundas Street any old day. John Street, Victoria Street, Dundas Street, Alfred Street, they make a paved canyon through which, disconcertingly, cars are driven, their tyres slip-slap-slapping against the wet granite. It was in this handsome but bleak chasm, with the wind knifing my ears, that I first laid eyes on George. He was still far off, and surprisingly coatless. He stepped up his pace and there was recognition in his movements. We strolled towards each other rather nervously, like gunslingers in a B-Western we decided later, grinning and then clasping.

'I heard somebody had arrived.'

'Last night,' I said. 'Where is your coat?'

There have been so many descriptions of his appearance, but to me he had the weathered tenderness of one of those vagrants whose face alters the day. A stranger, obviously myself, had been seen reading a book in the bar of the oilmen's pub the night before, 'So I knew it must be you.' I said that William Hazlitt had been jibed out of the inn at Winterslow for doing as much. George looked unwell yet sturdy, with ravaged features and with his thick dark curls whitening. He had huge, searching mariner's eyes and small neat hands which clearly did nothing except hold a biro or a pint. He was also in urgent need of sharing an indignity. Someone in the council office expected him to be able to do *anything*, but who could? He certainly could not. Someone had again 'drawn his attention' to the scandal of the giant hemlock in his patch, and how it was shedding its deadly seed. But they knew that he never went near his patch and that 'I don't know about such things.' Eventually they sent a council man to pull the hemlock up. We had reached 3 Mayburn Court, the address which had been in my book for years, and went to look at the patch, George with disgust. On the way I noted the small council flat above the ocean and the railed balcony where a convivial George would stand to give his Hitler impersonation. 'A terrific mimic', I had been told. At the door he said in all seriousness how lucky we were, 'You and I. Just think, if we hadn't been able to write, where would we be? I'll tell you where we'd be – on the dole. What else could we have done?' I said I would return at four and he went in.

I now did one of my favourite things, which is to reconnoitre an old town without a guide. George had resurrected Stromness's earlier name of 'Hamnavoe' in order for him to be flexible with Time, a way of writing which with him amounted to genius, and I too was alternately in Hamnavoe and Stromness as I wandered about. They doubled as a last port of call for the Greenland whalers, the Hudson Bay Company's vessels and Captain Cook. I stood by the wall a few steps from George's flat from which the convict ships drew their last water in Britain and noted how all the houses were built end-on to the sea so that they could escape the brute force of the easterlies. Gulls decorated their stepped gables. The long single street with several names was inspired by breakwaters, with closes every few yards which chop the might of gales and allowing only piercing fractions of them through. The town's Scandinavian origins persist in the mainly eighteenth century architecture. It was late summer and now and then burning, and now and then brilliantly cold. It was a town which bred men for the Canadian fur-trade, for fishing fleets and for the Navy. It was both as hard as nails and delicate, toil-driven and leisurely, rough and mannered – far northern, in short. It was evident at every step why a native poet had no driving reason to step much beyond it. Also it possessed an inexhaustible song – *The Orkneyinga Saga* – which served George as the *Odyssey* had served Derek Walcott.

Orkney is fortunate in the strength and variety of its continuities, its thousand year run of the best authors. From the saga writers (Icelandic actually) to Edwin Muir and George these seventy or so islands beyond the Pentland Firth have received no ordinary documentation, Probably no other British region has so eloquently retained its literary heart in such excellent working order. It was a Norse earldom until the 15th century. It is virtually tree-less due to the gales, and now almost heatherless because recent cornfields and market gardens have only been halted by the sea. The profusion of serene farms within wild scenery offer a domesticated yet unpredictable landscape. The chain of islands recede in all directions but with no view of the waters which separate them, suggesting that one could walk dry-foot to Shapinsay, Washington Irving's old home, or to Westray, where the Jacobites laid low. These waters are called sounds from the Old Norse *sund*, a narrow channel which flows between a greater and a smaller land. There is only one great country in Orkney and it is called Mainland. The Orcadians ride their sounds as Londoners do their buses, catching ferries here and there. It is a northern Aegean with Homer's gods and warriors in Viking parts. Blood-soaked, of course. The principal saint is Earl Magnus, done to death on Egilsay during the Easter of 1116 by his cousin Hakon's cook after Hakon's standard bearer had refused to carry out the execution. Soon afterwards, appalled by what he ordered, Earl Hakon, did the right thing and made a repentant journey to Jerusalem. Egilsay lies in its violent seas like a green arrow-head. The murder of Magnus has nourished its poetry. As a boy on Wyre, the little island at the foot of Egilsay, Edwin Muir could look across Rousay Sound and see the church which had been built at the scene of this crime. 'It was the most beautiful thing within sight, and it rose every day against the sky until it seemed to become a sign in the fable of our lives.'

Wyre was the smudge above Egilsay which I saw from the bedroom window after my first night in Orkney. Although by this time image after image of the islands had become scattered in my awareness as they were in the sea due to the eagerness of the young friend to show me as much as he could of the place before it became dark the previous evening. So far as I could tell, his car was leaping from island to island. This impressionism came to a halt at St. Magnus Cathedral, where he was organist. It is the colour of red sweet peas, a drenched dark pink moving towards dried blood, and it points up from Kirkwall like a towering memory. The poet-saint Earl Rognvald Kolsson built it in 1137 just twenty years after the murder of his uncle Earl Magnus, or rather half-built it, for there was a hiatus during the structure during which wind and rain roared through the unroofed interior, smoothing the carvings. Earl St Rognvald placed Earl St Magnus's bones high up in a column to the south of the altar where successively for almost a millennium they have been elevated by Masses and metrical psalms. The rosy cathedral is far more Norwegian than Scottish and indeed they say that it is the finest building in Scandinavia a great Norse church which draws the imagination like a fanned fire. We climb above its grandeur into what must be Kirkwall's lumber-room, for here are a great many broken or discarded objects, including the hangman's double ladder with it's thirteen rungs. 'Two goes up, one comes doon.' David the organist clatters down into the present and pulls out all the stops. Bach fills the chilly spaces. Huge tombstones have been brought in from the kirkyard and fixed to the aisle walls to prevent them from weathering. The music obscures the religious division and the light which in most countries would have died by now, stops fading. We are far north – Norse, in fact. There is a Westminster-style poets' corner and in the chancel some kind of compromise between the catholic and the civic, the Cathedral now being the property of the town council. Outside under the rare trees and at near to midnight one can see to read.

In bed I re-read a tale by George called 'The Seller of Silk Shirts' in which a Sikh boy has a successful day on Quoyaly and in which George is at his funniest. It is among my favourites, although where is Quoyaly? 'I am a Sikh boy. My name over here is Johnny.' George would have opened his front door to an Indian hawker, his case spilling ties. 'I have gone then to a house on a hill. Many hens promenade at the door. I have much fear of the dog but there are words in the inside darkness that say, "Down, Laddie, down."' I must not ask George where is Quoyaly? Nor why the inescapable litter of two world wars which everywhere draws my eye is ignored in his Orkney. The mess they left behind would at one time have driven to despair those who knew the islands before the military landed on them, though now it is less refuse than elegy. Thousands of soldiers, sailors and airmen, thousands of prisoners, all to make their mark. Nothing written in concrete is discreet. The word occupation is scrawled all over the land and on the sea itself. You cannot miss it, even if George does. What he leaves out is what obscures his vision. He celebrates Mass in cornfields, not on altars.

> *Our Lady of Cornstalks*
> *Our Lady of the Flail*
> *Our Lady of Winnowing*
> *Our Lady of Querns*
> *Our Lady of the Oven*
> *Blue Tabernacle*
> *Our Lady of the Five Loaves . . .*

In Kirkwall the Roman Catholic church stands where Junction Road becomes New Scapa Road. One mile to Scapa Flow says the signpost. It takes my breath away. One mile to the end of the Navy Race, and to where Orkney's battle detritus reaches its crescendo. Scapa Flow – that cold, tragic, enclosed water bristling with iron and sailor's bones. The surface is chopping, glittering and enigmatic, all slopping top and indifference to what it covers. Old battlefields specialise in this kind of negation, even if Scapa Flow is a battlefield without a fight, merely a depth into which a fleet can sink with or without all guns blazing. Crouching by the pier which serves the Flotta oilmen, I remember my first glimpse of this water. It is in a picture on the classroom wall, one of those character-forming reproductions of the day. A boy sailor mans his gun until his ship goes down and he drowns. Boy Somebody V.C. Or maybe it isn't Scapa after all but Jutland; it is hard to tell through time's havoc. There was definitely a drowned Scapa hero on Doreen's mantelpiece, her brother no less, who had gone down with the *Royal Oak* in 1940, and who would agree with Roy Fuller that

My photograph already looks historic,
The promising youthful face, the matelot's collar ...

I am not far from Marwick Head where the *Hampshire* went down, taking Lord Kitchener to Davy Jones, he whose pointing finger and glaring stare made millions volunteer. He was sailing to Russia to gip-up the laggards there. But even he is small-fry to Scapa's big catch, the Kaiser's seventy-five ironclads, his pride and joy, each vessel as fresh as paint and spit and polish could make it. Skeleton crews sank them all on a June morning in 1919, scrambling ashore to where I am now standing to watch them vanish. Great ladies had named them in champagne to fanfares and prayers, to bursting hearts and men's tears, the Empress, the arch-duchesses, the serene highnesses, all swimming patriotism, all making knots in the Navy Race. Who then could have imagined Scapa Flow? How indifferent it is. A drowned boy, a drowned warship, drowned hopes, the flecked bay is a tabula rasa shining but not reflecting anything other than a cold sky.

Later, in Stromness, an old woman calls me in out of the gale. Listening to my tale of Scapa, she says to her husband, 'Shall we show him the photos?' He nods feebly. But here he is looking like Lysander, having just surfaced from the German Grand Fleet with treasure in his hands, lovely marine instruments, somebody's water-logged belt. Beside him rise other youthful looters, naked and grinning, all with their trophies. It is a thirties Saturday. 'Only they put a stop to it. You get fined for treasure hunting now.' The woman had noticed me chatting to George in the street earlier on and mentions it, allowing what is known as a telling silence to follow. I am unable to interpret this. Unless it is on the lines of a prophet being honoured except in his own country. 'Show him the drawers,' orders the old man. So now I too am handling the Kaiser's stuff, a badge with locked eagles, a pretty plate from Dresden, a tin stamped Berlin.

Returning to Scapa with David the organist, we drive along the Churchill Barrier road which rides across hundreds of tremendous concrete blocks sprinkled between the islands like Oxos. After the sinking of the *Royal Oak* it had to be impossible for German U-boats to sneak into the Flow via the sounds of Lamb Holm, Glimps Holm, Burray and Ronaldsay. The blocks were made by Italian prisoners of war from the Western Desert. On the side the Italians made for themselves an enchanting chapel from a pair of Nissen huts and hundreds of bully-beef tins. The chapel stands on Lamb Holm and was the inspiration of a young soldier named Domenicho Chiccetti. We went in. Flowers, angels and saints throughout, and much holiness. A copy of Barabino's picture 'As a Fair Olive Tree in the Plains' rose above the altar, where Mass continues to be celebrated. Orkney, other than Hoy – 'High' – is all plains, plains afloat in sounds and firths, and with barely a fair tree.

Hoy looms up for miles around. I sail there in the morning on Mr Mowat's *Scapa Ranger*, a bouncy twelve-seater crammed with schoolchildren, twitchers and sturdy ladies engrossed in *The Orcadian*, the local paper for which George writes his weekly column called 'Under Brinkie's Brae' 'Walk to Rackwick. It is one of this world's best scenes', he advised me. We sail under the lee of a wartime block-ship. The air is nippy and the sea-birds scream. We are off Graemsay and I can now see the significance of Stromness as a provisioning last call for clippers and hulks. Stromness would have been the last of England, or home, for those en-route for Botany Bay and they would have watched the little town diminish with stricken gaze. To think that now, with our gaols so full, we have gone back to prison-ships. O for another Australia! Some are probably crying in the Home Office.

I land on Hoy and a packhorse path did indeed take me to one of this world's best scenes, but also to eloquent signs of its recent abandonment. One cannot live on beauty. Those who had struggled on Hoy for centuries fled during the Forties to Mainland and good soil. Their abandoned dry-stone houses in the given-up gardens come abruptly into view. Some had been seized back by those who no longer needed to plough or fish, people who had edged their way out of George's sight. In *Fishermen with Ploughs* he asks the uncomfortable question why 'the quality of life grows poorer as Progress multiplies its gifts on a simple community?' It is, of course, his main theme. It is why his poetry and stories are an inventory of what we have emptied out in order to make room for today's so-called essentials. We have thrown away many of the beautiful pared-to-the-bone objects which were so valuable – or labelled them By-gones and hung them round in the lounge-bar – each a form of treachery and tastelessness in his eyes. Hence the keen, sharp and restorative sentences of his evocations of a recent past. George has taught himself 'the shorthand of myth' such as that which the old Norse writers used, and it has created his style. From boyhood on, he heard at Rackwick the thin though rich song of the crofters such as had been sung by that turbulent water for a thousand years, then the unnatural silence which followed it as the singers were drawn to 'new altars'. They left behind the mighty uproar of the Rackwick sea and their rubbish, 'syrup tins, medicine bottles, bicycle frames, tattered novels, rubber boots, portraits of Queen Victoria'. Returning to Rackwick during his last years he tells himself that 'the great song must begin all over again, very far back, beyond the oxen and mill-stones and bronze throats of agriculture'.

Although aware of Peter Maxwell Davies having brought his song to Rackwick, I looked forward to hearing the pensive music which blows about the deserted habitation. What I had not bargained for was the monstrous uproaring of the cliffs, all taller and more chasmic even than Thomas Hardy's Beeney Cliff in Cornwall, and all in everlasting tumult as fulmars, guillemots and the Pentland Firth raged against them. I came to this stunning valley via the path below Ward Hill, Hoy's – or indeed Orkney's – Everest, picking a dry footing through ferns and rivulets. Rackwick itself struck a familiar chord for someone who had grown up in Suffolk during the farming depression and whose adventures took place in untenanted cottages and tumbling barns which were so derelict and rat-dwelt that the tramps making their way from spike to spike preferred a ditch to them.

At the end of *Fishermen with Ploughs*, a woman says, 'A host of cold voices greeted us in Rackwick – tern, skua, plover, lark, kittiwake, heron, diver, dotterel. Only the pigeons, though, come about the thresholds, looking for the old peace offering between man and dove, a crumb of bread. But till Conrad cuts our first harvest there's no bread to offer ... A hard existence though until the first harvest is cut in Rackwick. We eat boiled limpets and crabs till our guts loathe them.'

The highness of Hoy continues to restrict the kind of prosperity which has transformed Orkney at large. No longer on Mainland and most of the other isles that subsistence and its song. Instead, a cultivated view from shore to shore, and edge to edge greening of the land. Although George in his grieving way reminds his people of terrible losses, the small scale of the post-war expansion of the crops and the colourful openness – no hedges, low boundaries – does give a feeling of something blessed having taken place. Wheat, barley, pastures, flocks, herds, horses are all set out like the painted lead pieces of the toy farms in Mr Tricker's window and which, like meccano, you bought one at a time. Mainland had the whole set. But Hoy remains the reminder of what all these northern islands were like when George was born, somewhere 'To drudge in furrows till you drop'. East Anglia ditto. Walking to Rackwick by 'that mild mothering hill/and that chaste burn' criss-crossing the squelchy bits as one does on the great moors, careful not to catch up with the other day-excursionists from the *Scapa Ranger*, anxious not to be accosted by twitchers, regretting having arrived for just a few hours, I followed the track over Rora Head, striding along fast and meeting up with the Old Man in a sudden impact. There he was, all five hundred feet of him, tee-tering under the onslaught of winds and birds. One is usually on one's guard against the impact made by one's first glance of a famous object, hoping, I suppose, that one's response to it will be original. The Old Man is a dizzy pile of red sandstone bis-cuits balancing this way and that, and raucus like everything else with waves and kittiwakes. St Simeon Stylites, who eventu-ally increased the height of his pillar from a single step to forty cubits, would have surveyed the Old Man thoughtfully. Sailors from the naval base at Lyness would have come to look at him on their days off. A millennium hence a watcher may see him fall like dominoes, or Ozymandias. But now he pirouettes in his funnel of birds, safe as houses.

In the hierarchy of Hoy sights, the Dwarfie Stane comes second to the Old Man. It is a tomb-room cut out of a sandstone block during the third century BC and whose ceiling still shows the tool-marks. Who was laid to live again here? There are side rooms and the smell of damp stone perpetually encountering fresh air. And the door-stone fallen open. Nothing else. 'Inhabit me,' implores the Dwarfie Stane, but the visitor steps back.

George fills his warm room. There are rooms off it but this is the one he fills. He makes tea and brings it in. 'Mother's cups.' He cuts cake from the corner shop. The coal fire blazes as it does every day, winter and summer. I sit facing the dining-writing table and George sits by the hearth where, famously every afternoon, he 'interrogates silence.' But he is all for a talk now and I am struck by his facial resemblance to the poet James Turner, the concave features, the thick hair, the brilliant, drifting eyes. Tuberculosis marked both of them, separating them from the rest of us, making them fierce, determined – and delicate. Cracked lino curls up in a corner and a framed photo of George hangs lopsided by the door. There is the writer's mountain of books, a biro, a bit of writing-pad, some letters. Do I give myself a day a week for writing letters? This is the front room of a pensioner who likes a read. This is the home of an undomesticated man. This is the den of a man who has everything. We run on about this and that, with George re-filling the kettle and asking questions from the kitchen. We pass from Thomas Hardy to John Clare and then diffidently to George himself. He likes to explain how he works. He waits for the words to come to him. Every morning, with the breakfast pushed back to make a space, 'I sit there' – pointing – 'and if I'm lucky some words come. Just a few every day.' I mention Peter Maxwell Davies and the librettos. How is this done? He grins. 'Don't ask me. I don't do any of that – couldn't. He does it. He takes my words away with him and does it.' I tell him about my early writing days at Aldeburgh and about Ben Britten, which made me think of that sullen sea shifting the shingle, often listlessly and rarely roaring its head off as it does at Rackwick. George is pleased that I have seen Rackwick. 'Isn't it what I told you, the most beautiful place in the world?' Simply mentioning it makes him meditative. Should I leave? Did he want to work? Sleep? Interrogate? 'No, don't go. It is a treat.' So we dream by the blaze. 'Aren't we lucky to be able to do this? Write a bit then sit about the rest of the time.?' He repeats how that he has to wait for words to arrive in their right order, just a few every morning. The heat, the evident weariness, and this close-up for me of the experienced pacing of energy.

The natives of extraordinary places show weariness at the visitor's reactions, so I try not to bore George with my sightseeing. Returning from the kirkyard I did have to ask him about the Scottish custom of Hellenic monuments rising from Presbyterian graves, the draped granite urn on its tall plinth being a favourite. At Stromness scores of them stretch from the grass as if to be visible from the sea. He hadn't noticed. It was what a traveller would notice and was useful. But he had noticed, needless to say. Nothing had escaped him. In *Five Green Waves* there is a perfect account of the scene I had just left:

'I wandered away from him among the branching avenues of tomb-stones – the tall urns and frozen angels of modern times; the fiery pillars with the names of grandfathers on them; the scythe-and-hourglass slates of the eighteenth century; the lichened leprous tombs of a still earlier age. This small field was honeycombed with the dead of generations – farmers with stony faces; young girls rose-cheeked with consumption; infants who had sighed once or twice and turned back to the

94

darkness; stern Greek-loving ministers; spinsters with nipped breasts and pursed mouths. I stood on the path, terrified for a moment at the starkness and universality of shrouds; at the infinite dead of the island, their heads pointing westwards I a dense shoal, adrift on the slow tide that sets towards eternity.'

George takes the opportunity to talk shop. Do I have an agent? No, he does not have an agent. Reviewing. 'They (*The Glasgow Herald*) send me something now and then.' He makes the fire up, makes another pot of tea, asks for news, saying, 'I put something down every day, although it may not be much. Do you do that?' My head is drumming with marvels, but am reserved about my walk to Maes Howe in its flowery meadow off the Stromness-Finstown road. A party of 'Jerusalem-farers,' or young Norse-crusaders, had taken shelter from bad weather in this superb Neolithic rites of passage room, in which every stone exactly fits, and they scribbled on its walls such things as 'Many a proud woman has had to enter here stooping.' The caretaker from the neighbouring cottage had made me go first. Another rune says – George's translation – 'Ingibiorg is the loveliest of the girls.' This room was already three and a half thousand years old when the Jerusalem farers sheltered here in 1151 and scribbled in their feathery hand. Nothing totally disappears in Orkney and the line between pre-history and written history is a faint one. From Ingibiorg's boys to the circle of the sun, or the Ring of Brogar. Calm planks of split flagstones, their tops shaped like scimitars, and their subsidiary circle the Stones of Stenness stand by two glittering lochs. Flotillas of swans pass below a monolith called the Watch Stone. The banks of the lochs are covered with what looks like sheet-celandine, so dense are the burnished heads. All around lie the long-dead. The four archaeologists are very much alive and are only about a foot down. There is a hand-carved stone ditch. Twenty-seven of the original stones are erect and one is covered with Victorian graffiti by the men with Orkney place-names. '*Always by the shore,*' wrote George,

> *Kirk and kirkyard*
> *Legends of men, their carved names*
> *Faced east, into first light, among sea sounds.*

Hugo brought him to Oxford to convalesce after the operation. For George, it must have been like getting better on the moon.

His final *Under Brinkie's Brae* column in the *Orcadian* on 3 April 1996 warned,

'There is a price to be paid for Progress; already the 'tabs' are being shown us, one after another.'

His Requiem Mass was sung thirteen days later in St Magnus's Cathedral, on the feast day of the saint. His last written words were in praise of April, 'the month that tastes of childhood.'

At the funeral Peter Maxwell Davies played his 'Farewell to Stromness'. Back home, in another world about which he liked to read, I found his present, and read *House of Winter,*

> *It is a bitter house. On the step*
> *Birds starve.*
> *The sign over the door is warped and faded.*
>
> *Inside one chamber, see*
> *A bare thorn.*
> *Wait. A bud breaks. It is a white rose.*
>
> *We think, in the heart of the house*
> *A table is set*
> *With a wine jar and broken bread.*

Mountainous Encounters

I was grown-up before I saw mountains and they remain for me an adult experience. There also remains the puzzle that whilst I accept East Anglian land as level, I do not regard it as low in the Scottish and Dutch sense. Due to the keen climate, East Anglians regard themselves as elevated, plateau-raised. But the North Sea does not. It slides into and over us whenever it has a mind to, and at areas like the aptly named Wash it blurs the distinction between land and water. And even where we have cliffs, they are like short pastry, crumbing in the mouth of the slightest flood. So why am I not a Netherlander? Why, like the rest of Suffolk and Norfolk, do I act and breathe as a native of the high ground? When I first went to Wales and walked through the mountain passes, I was stunned by the beauty, the bulk, the sheer non-utilitarian wastefulness, but I seemed to encounter a familiar air.

I remember my first big mountain exposure distinctly. My brother and I had been staying in Myddle, Shropshire when, meandering on and on in our little old car, we found ourselves at the feet of Cader Idris. I say 'at the feet' because the first glimpse of this mountain leaves one surprised and supplicant. I filed it away for exploration, for getting to know it, indeed for daring to get to know it later on. On and on we drove, and Cader Idris too vast to pass, so that it darkened the car, yet at the same time threw a brilliance all around us. We saw farms and cottages and wondered how anyone could live with it. This, perhaps, is the distinction between the plateau-landers and the mountain-landers, the ability to live where rock soars and echoes, and becomes a blocking-out of nearby distances. Mountains lift the eyes, plains narrow them.

Some years later, I did live with Cader Idris, just for a few days. An old friend, Derek Richards, had been made Rector of Arthog and his fine house lay perpetually in its shade, as clearly intended by some Georgian clergyman. Below the rectory spread the Mawddach estuary and across this stalked the Great Western Railway's wooden mile of bridge linking Arthog to Barmouth. During the summer of 1876, Gerard Manley Hopkins and some of his Society of Jesus colleagues were given leave to take a holiday in Barmouth and they travelled along the line to the opposite end of the bridge, with Cader Idris directly before them. They lived uncomfortably at St Asaph in the Clwyd valley, in a Gothic religious house 'like Lancing done worse.' Hopkins half-considered converting the Welsh from Wesleyism, then decided no. Barmouth, he told his mother, was a perfectly safe spot, drains-wise, 'with nothing worse than this, that the town empties its sewage, like other well-watered shores, into Neptune's salt-wash.' Returning to Arthog, I saw the poet paying his penny toll to walk across the bridge, his eyes fixed on Cader Idris. Back at St. Asaph he was amused by the Society's mountainous garden, which was 'all heights, terraces, Excelsiors, misty mountain tops, seats up trees called Crows' Nests, flights of steps seemingly up to heaven lined with burning aspiration upon aspiration of scarlet geraniums; it is very pretty and airy but it gives you the impression that if you took a step farther you would find yourself somewhere on Plenlimmon.' The shadowy Arthog garden made no such effort. It preserved a terraced decency on such levels as it could find below the Idris foothills and the house itself turned its back on the heights and looked down towards Barmouth Bay, and through tall plantations. Most of the houses along the Dolgelley road were similarly arranged in heavily wooded gardens and small parks, like people who place a hand over the eyes to concentrate on what they require from a view, and no more. Hopkins, with his chilly St. Beauno's College and his warm feelings for the Welsh, and notwithstanding the rule of his order, saw through and past domesticated Wales to 'what gives me a rise of the heart.' This was Snowdon itself. Priests should keep their eyes lowered and look away from whatever it was that could distract them. Hopkins found nature wildly distracting. It was forever catching his eye, filling him with desire. It was against the Rule.

The old Welsh poets thought of Idris as a giant intellect, thus making it possible for people to dwell in his titanic shadow rationally and unthreatened. Did Hopkins and his holiday-making Jesuits climb, as I did, high above the Arthog orchards and parks to the first of those knowledgeable sills of volcanic rock which, after surprisingly little walking and clambering, brought me to the summit? Scattered sheep farms, the sad cries of animals and endless tracks were a reminder that however upward I pressed, I would still be in my friend's parish. Ancient folds and giddy runs of drystone walling were evidence of community. Some kind of living had been dragged out of Cader Idris immemorially.

There are still many routes to its pinnacles, all of them spectacular, each of them with its own message, its own views. From the south there are paths from Tal-y-Lyn, Dolcae and Abergwmlyn. Or one can climb up via tracks at each end of the main range, the one which leads from Cross Foxes or that which leads from just by Bird Rock. But the quickest way is via the Minfford road, and the easiest way is by the Pony Track from Dolgellau.

The latter has been for centuries Cader Idris's pilgrim's way. Or you can take the Fox's Path, a crueller journey over broken stone and the coldest spring water in Wales. My way, rather like Hopkins's imaginary climb out of St Beauno's College garden straight on to Plynlimon, rose from Arthog itself, a lovely beginning, all Victorian gardens, rhododendron shrubberies, peacocks and hidden crashing streams. And thus to the ultimate rewards of Cader Idris, which are the corrie lakes on the summit of Pen-y-Gader, one in its north cwm and the other in its southern cwm. The latter, Llyn-y-Cau, is the subject of Richard Wilson's haunting painting in the National Gallery, and is one of the most extraordinary features of British geography. Wilson's interpretation of this lonely corrie is personal and strange. He has been criticised for allowing Attic shepherds to pipe in the foreground of his pastoralised jagged scene, and by painting a Welsh mountain lake so that it looks like Vesuvius filled with water. As a Montgomeryshire man, though, for whom the blackness of mountains would have been a fact of life, he may have had the opposite notion, that Cader Idris, as the seat of philosophy and poetry, was in line with Olympus when he worked on this celebrated landscape. Cader's exterior may have been the peaks of enlightenment – but inside! Inside lived Gwyn an Nadd, lord of the underworld. Gwyn with his pack of hounds called the Cwn Annwn, with which he rounded-up the souls of the new dead and shepherded them into the Shades. Mythically, this is a mountain which instructs us, of the Welsh at least, how to live and where to disappear. Richard Wilson knew this.

Even as I set out on a good morning for the tip of Cader Idris, I knew I was on the way to seeing much further than Worcestershire and Ireland, which is the view offered by Pen-y-Gader (3,100 feet), its highest peak. I was made insecure by the patent insecurity of those who inhabited this range for three thousand years and left their piled stones, which cannot be dated, as evidence. The mountain's return for humanity's respect for it – there has never been any attempt to capture it entire for agriculture or quarrying, or whatever – is to show a certain benignity to the settlements around its feet. Or even, here and there, up to its very brow. The companionableness of the vanished herdsmen and their families hangs around the myriad tracks, even if it gives a hollow retort by the abandoned hearths, some Neolithic, some nineteen-twenties or later. Arthog will always remain for me the gate to the knowledge of these rearing pastures. Weird to think that just over a century ago it was also the gate to Britain's own gold rush. No mountain tops for the miners from Cornwall and even *the* goldrush lands of Australia and California, when the Mawddach valley was mistakenly thought to be more or less solid with gold. Twenty-four mines were opened between Barmouth and Clogau, and just enough gold was extracted to make a crown for the Prince of Wales in 1911, and wedding rings for Queen Mary and the Princess Royal – and for quite a few Welsh brides. Where locals and foreigners alike scrambled for a fortune are noiseless glades. The polluted salmon stream now runs diamond pure under miles of conifer. At Maescwm, the Forestry Commission has brought together many of the aquatic plants which cool the vale, along with the not wholly satisfactory request:

> *Leave nothing but footprints,*
> *Take nothing but pictures,*
> *Kill nothing but time.*

'Let those kill time who like it better dead,' as Rose Macaulay remarked.

I climbed Tyran Mawr. The views there, they said, were even better than from Cader. Below lay the old grass track known as the Black Road. It was probably Roman in origin and it ran in a loop round the west bastion of Tyran Mawr, and then went on winding all of the seven miles to the Dysynni Valley, making a fabulous walk. Below, too, glowered the Crogenen Lakes which, like all corrie lakes, are too deep and still for comfort. The Crogenen Lakes were 800 feet up and the hard head of Tyran Mawr itself an eagle height of over two thousand feet above the sea. One of the lakes had an island covered with larches, the other a white edge which dipped and shrieked as hundreds of gulls rode in its shallows. There was barking and shouting. A shepherd and his twisting, racing dogs were seeing the flock down. There was, as on Cader, sweet shrill birdsong. Tyran Mawr echoed all this whilst at the same time keeping hold on its own quietness. I saw below what looked like the photographic negative of a lost city taken from the air. Properly focused, it became an acre of burnt gorse. Descending, I was now and then positioned to stare into chimney-pots, and once, through cracked slates, into the unique void which is provided by an abandoned Welsh chapel. There hung the galleries where the Victorian goldminers sang of golden Jerusalem, golden corn and golden gates. Cardigan Bay, coming and going in the mist, seemed to belong to another sphere altogether.

Back home and sheltered from the demands made by immense views, I tried to see Cader Idris and the North Wales mountains as the Jacobean traveller would have seen them, by poring over Speed's maps from his spectacular *The Theatre of Great Britain,* a atlas of the old scenic attitudes as well as of this island in 1610. John Speed is a demoter of mountains, a carto-grapher who takes them down a peg or two, who wishes they were not there. He calls Cader Idris Cardoridrie Hill and most of the Welsh mountains nothing at all. Contourless, his draw-ing of them on his charts create a pustulate situation for those unfortunate enough to live among them. They regretfully swell up all over the place, being 'very high and very many', and are 'uneven to travel.' In Brecon the aldermen told him how impos-sible it was to throw anything off one of their mountains. Cloaks, hats and sticks hurled from it 'would never fall, but were with the air and wind still returned back.' Mountains in Radnorshire made the soil hungry and churlish. But mountain-ous Merioneth is worse, where 'the air for great pleasure, nor soil for great profit' cannot be recommended, and where 'the spired hills cluster together so near and so high, that shepherds upon their tops, falling at odds in the morning, and challenging the field for a fight, before they can come together to try out the quarrel, the day will be spent, and the heat of their fury shut up with their sheep.' It was a relief to come to Flintshire, where there was 'nothing mountainous' and no height for sons of 'bad angels' to stare down on to good men. And then there is Snowdon-Hill, doyen of a range which may 'not unfitly be termed the British Alps.' The Welsh tell tall stories 'and I think the Reader had rather believe them than go to see whether it be so or no.' Quite. He liked Anglesey, where' the air is reasonably grateful', and where he didn't have to draw a great many humps.

It was an Anglesey friend who took me to meet Olwen Caradoc Evans, map-finder extraordinary. We crossed the Menai Strait to find her and from then on it was all mountains until I grew directionless. For inhabitants of the undulate plain, who can identify rise or two, are lost in mountain passes. It was hot

summer and the lofty snow shone blue. Olwen's house was bois-
terous with dogs and full of charts, maps and 'tours'. She had
been the friend of H. V. Morton whose '*In the Steps of* ...' tours
were beloved of my mother, but which I had never read. Olwen
followed every footstep through Wales, but via cartography. She
gave me a glorious chart of the Welsh coast, the St. George's
Channel area, made by Lewis Morris for the Lords of the Admi-
ralty in 1737–1744, and indeed presented by the author to their
Lordships ' with the greatest submission.' Mountains do not rise
up like paps or dugs on this coast, or any natural feature which
might deflect utilitarian labour. It is a chart which sets the Welsh
to work, on land or at sea. The cartouche is a whirl of fishing,
husbandry, mining,' timber falling,' ship building and woollen
manufactory. A nude Neptune with seaweedy pubic hair lolls in
the bullrushes. Compass course is set for the year 1748. The true
meridian touches Bardsey, where the saints lie in their thousands. We sink into Olwen's library. It is unbearable to leave
even to eat. What grows certain is that the Welsh and their
mountains have been under perpetual observation. Travellers
have left notes on what they have seen all over Britain but never
with quite the same nosiness as when they went back to Wales.

Back on Anglesey, staying with my old friend John Williams-
Hughes, I heard a nice example of Welsh come-back to English
inquisitiveness. It concerned Borrow, needless to say. George
Borrow, whilst writing *Wild Wales*, had stayed in John's house.
Returning from a fact-finding tramp, he saw a boy mending the
roof and addressed him in Welsh. The boy replied in French.
Borrow was floored. 'You,' said the lad, 'speak to me in a language which is not your own, so I answer you in a language
which is not my own.'

John's house had just been inherited from his mother, who

had died in her nineties. It was one of those houses pounced upon these days by time-warpists and left as it is down to the ossified crumbs in the biscuit barrel. I never met Mrs Williams-Hughes, J.P. but years of hearing about her provided a repressive image. Her son, a world traveller, submitted to her sway the moment he opened her front gate. Her calling stones still lay in the porch. Each friend left a stone of distinctive shape and hue to show that they had called. 'Too scared to knock?' I asked John. 'Often,' he said. He gave me her bedroom, sweet with old lady. Her ancient hairs were in the silver-backed brush and her Bible, filled with celluloid texts as markers, lay on the bedside table. There was a vast satin eiderdown, icy to the touch. Creeper tapped on the window. I saw John's father for the first time, in his bird's-eye maple frame. There were thick, clean, starched sheets and pillows like feather mountains. 'You should be comfortable here,' John said. We had been walking across Red Wharf Bay to see the ribs of old boats, and sand tumbled from my socks. I didn't like to read Mrs Williams-Hughes's Bible for fear of losing her place and wished that I had borrowed one of Olwen's books. 'The Shepherd Boy of Snowdon Hill', perhaps. 'Of course we have mountains on Anglesey,' said John. 'We shall climb them in the morning.' I dreamed of his mother on the bench handing down the most the law could offer, and lining up her calling-stones.

The following days we alternately drove and walked across Mona, as Anglesey was called before the English named it their island. Every five miles or so we called on one or other of John's cousins, doctors, widows, an actress, a solicitor, and eventually a bard.

The bard lived in a bungalow with picture-windows, so that the afternoon rugby on television looked like fleas scuttling

around in a bowl compared with the scenery outside. The room
was full of bardic chairs and bardic crowns in a glass case. And
there was a room full of bardic poetry. The rugby finished and
we had high tea. I enquired about the poetry, gently and sin-
cerely, not wishing to sound like yet another nosey-parker in
Cambria. But the bard said that I would not be capable of
understanding it even if he could explain it. But there it was, on
the shelves, all the poetry. He opened the glass case with a little
key, withdrew a silver crown and placed it on my head. It felt
delightful; one can see why people like wearing crowns. He and
John and the bard's wife talked Welsh whilst I read a gazetteer
and sat mesmerised by the view. 'Yes,' said the bard's wife 'we
managed to get ourselves a good view!'

She complained of 'him' filling the house up with bardic
chairs. Soon there wouldn't be room to move. Why, I ration-
alised, wasn't the same chair and the same crown used each
time? And I cited Westminster Abbey. They all three looked
puzzled. 'Oh no,' said the bard's wife 'you get the chair *and* the
crown.'

The next day, making sure that no cousins were around, John
and I swam naked in the Irish sea and worse, drank bottled beer
in Mrs Williams-Hughes's drawing room. 'I will show you her
grave before you leave,' said John. As we had entered the house
he had glanced out of habit at the calling-stones and observed,
'Mrs Roberts has been.' I could see what made some men world
travellers.

It was Owen Thomas who showed me the Black Mountains.
He himself lives on a chapel-crowned hill which is nearly a
mountain outside Caerphilly. His house was the manse and it
retains a certain strength and seriousness. Below at night Caerphilly blinks and glitters like Babylon. Just across the lane from

the house is Handel's sheep farm, mucky by Suffolk standards and full of cries. Owen is a musician and a linguist, a little man with a strong voice. Like the Cornish, and unlike East Anglians, the Welsh speak with a decided resonance, and more so when they speak to each other. Could this be because of the wind and the high wild places? Or is it due to some element in their language? Owen had only recently learned to drive when we set off for Llantony and the Black Mountains, which are made of Old Red Sandstone. If the Black Mountain scarps and outcrops are precipitous and frightening, their valleys and seclusions must be among the earth's most benign and blessed spots. We walked the four miles from Llantony to Capel-y-ffin where Father Ignatius had at last managed to set up an Anglican version of the Benedictine Order. He was a deacon in his early thirties, seven years older than Gerard Manley Hopkins, and in a far greater dilemma due to his Catholic teaching in a Protestant milieu. Poor Father Ignatius, alias the Reverend Joseph Lyne, had scandalised East Anglia and fled to the holy Black Mountains. His mesmeric preaching and beautiful face combined, plus his genuine spirituality, brought him converts and the wrath of the establishment. His ordination, towards the end of his life, by Joseph Vilatte, an 'Old Catholic' bishop, was what the law would term 'unsatisfactory.' Kilvert had climbed to Capel-y-ffin to glimpse the strange brotherhood building its monastery with the help of masons and was so sorry for the young monks having to dig the foundations dressed in long robes and sandals. Down below in Clyro he made friends with Father Igantius's family who made the Swan Inn their base when they came to see him. Eventually it would be the masons, as it were, in the shape of Eric Gill and his community who would succeed the sacred diggers. Owen and I sat in the little chapel and contemplated the overlay of its relics, the faded furnishings of the unofficial Benedictines, the handprints of the freely loving Gill.

If you have mountains in your back-yard you will have strangers in your sights or in your hair. During the 1870's the Welsh were so revivalist in their valleys that few would have known about such high goings-on as Gerard Manley Hopkins in the steep garden at St. Asaph, and his contemporary in the Black Mountains. Walking from Clyro to Hay I understood the dominance of Francis Kilvert. It was his bent road, his Wye riverside, his glorious red sandstone wall ahead. There were days when the spectacle could not be equalled 'not even by the high Alpes.' There were times when he could have cried with excitement, and when he longed for someone to admire it with him. 'A man came whistling along the road riding upon a cart horse. I would have stopped and drawn his attention to the mountains but I thought he would probably consider me mad. He did not seem to be the least struck by or to be taking the smallest notice of the great sight' The whistling man's indifference and the clouding day quenched the transfiguration. 'Soon all was cold and grey and all that was left of the brilliant gleaming range was the dim ghostly phantom of the mountain rampart scarce distinguishable from the greying sky.'

In the poetry of R. S. Thomas there are hills but not mountains. His most profound hills are those which back the empty cross of the Pieta. His Welsh hills are the work places of the mean-minded, the scrabblers at life. The latter are also pitiful because they do not look up. He and I once sat together in an Ipswich pub, having supper and waiting to read our work at a festival. He had driven all the way from Aberdaron to Suffolk in one go, and his strength was noticeable. His face was lean, fleshless and severe, his manners a kind of remembered consideration. Owen had once taken me to see his church, but I knew that I should not confess this. Or my impressions and opinions of Wales. Or even that I had bought his books, from *The Stones of the Field* on. During the reading a voice called out, 'Can you read a little louder, sir?' There was a gasp from the cognizant like the shock-horror of the characters in a Bateman drawing, before Thomas answered 'No, sir' and went on reading as before. I tried to hear him taking matins in St Hywyn's, uninterrupted, careful not to hurt with his understanding of bitterness.

'Do you know Wales?' he asked in the pub. 'No,' I said, truthfully.

A Plantation House

As is so often the case, I am travelling for one purpose but with
the hope that I will find time for another en route. Flying to
North Carolina to give talks at a festival, I intend to do a little
work on the playlet about Julian of Norwich which has been
rashly promised for Chelmsford Cathedral. North Carolina,
these old English cities, this ancient woman, how remote they
all are, and especially when pondered upon from a New York
plane. We descend upon a Southern state apparently entirely
made of leaves. A clearing arrives, and oven-ready concrete.
Raleigh. They told me it would be baking, Raleigh, the poet-
captain's very own capital of a country in which he never set
foot. Beyond Raleigh, the endless forests which are having their
scents burned out of them. Sir Walter's men would have been
sniffing the Carolinas from their decks afar off, their bodies suddenly excited by the approaching exotica.

We were late getting going in America. Having discovered it
at the beginning of the 16th century, we did not start to lay
claim to it until the 1580's. Even then the Queen was tepid,
although she did say 'Call it Virginia after us.' She meant America. Coming down, with the anti-panic music faint as the pipes
of fairyland in my drumming ears, I fix myself to the window,
thinking that I might spy Roanoke Island. On the eve of the
Epiphany 1585 Queen Elizabeth knighted Raleigh, whom she
had found in his younger days very attractive, and who she now
found possibly very useful. He had told her that not only should
they claim the New World but settle it with people from the old

one. A novel notion. Colonisation became all the talk at court, along with dispiriting thoughts that England may have had its day. There was talk of paradise now and not after death. The Queen's mind was filled with loot, with her ships down to the gunnels with the weight of gold. Although Roanoke Island proved to be a dismal beginning for England-over-the-Ocean, it did provide it with a haunting mystery, one which hasn't been solved to this day. Which is why I longed to catch a glimpse of a twelve-mile strip of earth spread out in the shallows before North Carolina proper filled the view. Virginia Dare, granddaughter of a Devon brickie, was born in Roanoke, the first English-American. What a good name for such a girl; you couldn't have made it up.

Nor was the first governor of an American settlement the kind of person one might expect but an artist named John White, who made a wonderful watercolour record of what he found in his 'state.' His exquisite pictures of Indians and natural history contrast greatly with the clumsy black and threatening wood-block illustration of books back home, and although he did not paint his fellow English settlers, his 'view' of the natives and their world is so percipient that his tinted drawings convey a far more advanced understanding of America than anything logged by sea-captains and fortune hunters. White painted anthropology and could future colonists have only learned from his approach to the question of how to behave when the land you intend to claim is already in some kind of ownership, many barbarities might have been spared. He saw Roanoke interestingly occupied, an island where there were no 'heathens', only a different idea of the sacred. He saw plants and insects and native creatures, and he made the first drawing of a banana. His album is unsuperstitious, his eye scientific, his artistic skill that of a first-rate illustrator of the best textbooks of any age. With White in charge, England's first footing on America should have been firm enough, but having planted his fellow emigrants, he had to return for London for supplies and to report to the Queen and to Sir Walter. All this taking three years.

White's homecoming to Roanoke was terrible. It began with him and the others from the ship approaching the settlement with 'many familiar tunes of Songs', and looking forward to them being taken up by their friends in the wooden English village which had been planted on such hopeful soil, but instead there was silence. Not a soul, not a sound. But soon, on a post, carved in 'fayre Capitall letters' they read CROATOAN and on a tree carved in 'faire Roman letters' they read CRO. This was the name of an island which belonged to the once-friendly Indians who had modelled for White. He should have gone there to find out what had happened to his colony, to ask where everybody was, but some complicated naval business made any further investigation of what had occurred impossible, or so he said, and therefore he sailed back to England. Some eight years later, in a letter to Richard Hakluyt, White wrote the first words of what is now known as 'The Mystery of the Lost Colony,' a drama which intrigues the United States to this day.

'Thus you may plainly perceive the success of my fifth and last voyage to Virginia, which was no less unfortunately ended than frowardly (perversely) begun, and as luckless to many as sinister to myself ...'

As well as 'Croatoan' on a post, White had found 'about the place many of my things spoiled and broken, and my books torn from the covers, the frames of some of my pictures and maps rotten and spoiled with rain, and my armour almost eaten through with rust ...'

Harry and Eva Phillips are at Raleigh to meet me. The airport tarmac sizzles. They are Jewish doctors who have been up-rooted from two continents before finding a haven in a third. We drive to Chapel Hill where their house hides in trees from the sun. Not only is it shadowy and cool but, to an East Anglian, downright chilly when it came to going to bed and I long to let in some of the hot night air. I listen to whippoor-wills, the American nightjar, for the first time. I lie on the bed and go over Harry and Eva's long trek to where they feel most comfortable, the route being to some degree a classic twentieth century one. Flight from the pogroms in Lithuania and Russia, flight again from South African apartheid in 1956 – 'We could not bring four children in the Cape surrounded by such poli-tics.' – and so flight to Sir Walter Raleigh-land via Boston, two brave old doctors wise beyond words, and in their wake racist louts of all nations. It is near midnight and they are swimming naked in their pool. A paroxysm of shyness such as has not overcome me since boyhood caused me to turn down their invitation to join them. I hear splashes and words and the lone callings of the whippoorwills, then make a start on Dame Julian.

'After this I saw with my own eyes in the face of the crucifix hanging before me and at which I was ceaselessly gazing something of his pas-sion. I saw insults and spittle and disfiguring and bruising, and lin-gering pain more than I know how to describe: and there were frequent changes of colour. On one occasion I saw that half his face, from side to centre, was covered with dry blood, and that afterwards the other half was similarly covered, the first half clearing as the second half came.

All this I saw physically, yet obscurely and mysteriously ... So I saw him and sought him; I had him and wanted him. It seems to me that this should be an experience common to all .'

The following evening Harry and Eva take me to Duke University to meet the others. The festival to commemorate the New World is about to start. First, dinner in hall, so we have to put our suits on. Or so says the programme. We honoured guests from England, Stephen Spender, D. M. Thomas and other luminaries. I see Stephen and Denis seated at the far end of a mighty nineteen twenties' medieval hall, looking spruce but disconsolate. Trays of coke and hamburgers are awry before them, and they too sit awkwardly having, like me, arranged themselves for some kind of high table. I gawp around and Denis grins, 'This is it,' in his jolly Cornish voice. Harry and Eva are now in the Durham cinema, having dropped me off, and so do not witness our gloom. Half a dozen students in T-shirts and baseball caps rollick in the cafeteria. A festival man comes to calm us down and to say that we had read too much into 'Dinner' and that our formal reception would be later. It now being six-thirty we crave for alcohol, so the very worried organiser takes us to a down-town bar, imploring us not to stay long or drink more than one whatever it is. Denis is joyful, Stephen bone-weary and I am less thirsty than ravenous. Back at Duke, the welcome party deserves our suits and we recover from our first impressions and are taken through myriad introductions, clasped, patted and made much of in the heartfelt American manner. Afterwards, I help Stephen to find his room, noting his exhaustion. He looks over-weight and crumpled, a towering figure with a big tummy uncomfortably strapped-in by a slipping belt and hot glistening skin. He has been visiting Christopher Isherwood and Don Bachardy on the West Coast. His room turns out to be a just-vacated student's cell. The narrow bed gives a little scream when he collapses on it. He makes no complaint. Indeed, he is saintly. But he must have a bathroom. The nearest one is passages and stairs away. Realising that Stephen is a man who has to have his complaining done for him, I find the organiser and declare without more ado that ' I am so sorry, but Sir Stephen's accommodation is not suitable and he must, you will understand, go to an hotel.' ' Why not, why not!' Off he runs. Stephen thanks nobody for this. During the transference, noting the florid tiredness, the accepting blue gaze, the bundled-together luggage, and what could be the cumulative effect of years of academic lecture-rooms, I see Stephen Spender as one of those writers who have condemned themselves to a Dante-esque circuit of lectures and readings which must continue until he hasn't the strength to climb aboard a plane. A huge audience came to hear him talk on 'D. H. Lawrence as I knew him,' and was flattened when, without warning or change of poster, he switched to something like 'Education and Marxism.' All through the festival he, Denis Thomas and myself, crossed each other's paths, Denis baring his wicked teeth and muttering, 'The girls, the girls!' like a boy given the run of a sweetshop.

Between these official functions, Harry, Eva and I go for walks in Durham, a city which started life as a railroad halt, but had soared into grandeur and tobacco money. Immense quantities of it. The cost of all the public buildings scarcely made a dent in it. Members of the Duke family were still in residence, so to speak, and whether their status was being undermined or destroyed by today's anti-smoking habits it was impossible to find out. Their factories were being changed into shopping malls and restaurants, their tobacco fields partly abandoned – although this was no new thing, as tobacco crops made the soil unfit for corn, and tobacco-ruined earth is a normal sight in North Carolina. Absolutely un-ruined were the Greco-Roman art galleries, libraries, and state architecture generally. Duke University itself is superbly classical, not a million dollars spared where a million dollars were needed. How strange that Raleigh should have brought tobacco home to England and that his American state – although he was never anywhere near it – should have given birth to the American Tobacco Company.

Sitting in Harry and Eva's resinous garden at Chapel Hill with the bell notes of the southern birds echoing in the woods, I confess to never smoking, though for no good reason. I tried hard but with no success. They fetch a wartime snapshot album of themselves, and there they are, the newly-married pair of them in their houseman's white coats outside a London hospital, puffing away. Though not now, not for a long time. We could visit the farmhouse where old Washington Duke and his son Buck, broke after the Civil War, scratched a living from selling the local bright-leaf from a cracked wagon in their yard. They tied the bright-leaf up into bags labelled Pro Bono Publico. And who, looking at municipal and academic Durham could deny it? And how ironic that it was Sir Walter's monarch King James who insisted upon the first non-smoking area. Bringing bright-leaf into his kingdom might well have been one of the many reasons for James's dislike of Raleigh. Next to their beauty, what the king liked in his men was sweet breath. In his furious *A Counterblaste to Tobacco* he wrote, 'Herein is not only great vanity, but a great contempt of God's good gifts, that the sweetness of man's breath, being a good gift from God, should be wilfully corrupted by this stinking smoke.' Sir Walter was then in the Tower, though not for smoking, and there he, poet-founder of the New World, would remain for thirteen, dragging years, until James's lust for gold let him out so that he could search for Eldorado. James should have forgiven Raleigh his tobacco for writing his marvellous *History of the World* for Prince Henry. Had Prince Henry succeeded James there may not have been civil war, but he died at eighteen, the prince of promise. Sir Walter would have told him about Roanoke Island and the whippoorwills and magnolias which touched the sky.

Harry, Eva and I continue to explore Durham in the now tolerable heat. Dukal parks, Dukal museums and on the West Campus, the Duke Chapel with 'seventy-seven inspirational stained-glass windows and a two hundred and ten feet bell-tower patterned after that at Canterbury Cathedral, and with a half-million dollar Flentrop organ.' Raleigh's town on Roanoke would have patterned itself on somewhere like Bideford or Exmouth, so far as it could, plus extra close-fencing. It would have been a ghetto planted among Governor White's Indian models. Presumably, the Indians found this impossible. Did they carry the colony away into the sunny, scented depths of the interior and make them take their thick dirty clothes off and become civilised like them? There was no evidence of massacre, only of desertion.

The British-American Festival over, a young Raleighian carries me off to Caswell County. It is a planned surprise. Where and who in Caswell County? His non-air-conditioned car does a slow fifty along empty roads and his arm juts from the window as in films. He is grinning and secretive and I feel captured. I don't know what has happened to Spender and Thomas but after the ' surprise' I am to stay with a Dr Blythe, no relation, and then return to Harry and Eva. It is all arranged. 'You wait!' says the driver. He has a fine head, just right for one of John White's anthropological portraits. I make guesses. 'We are going to Virginia?' 'Very nearly.' After some forty miles we turn sharp right, and there it stands, my first antebellum mansion in its park, all white columns and clapboarding. The approach is like the opening of a novel, with the lovely house gradually introducing itself in the now half-dark evening. There is box-hedging. Willow-oaks and apparitional magnolias stand in great clumps. The owner of the house, who is in the secret, stands smiling in the porch. Nobody welcomes a guest like a certain kind of American. The driver leaps from the car as they do in the movies and runs and kisses her. ' Here he is!' I am awed by the magnificence. The secret is explained. A Suffolk friend has been sending my books to this house. My host herself has been there. 'How is Blythburgh? ... Bury St. Edmunds?' The next day both she and the driver have to leave, and they hand over the house to me. 'Do anything you like for a few days. There will be somebody to cook your dinner ... somebody to take you to Raleigh airport.'

Now I am in a kind of stranded silence, one which is quite unlike that at home and upon which everybody remarks. I explore my realm and find a Confederate soldier buried under the front lawn, the son of the house brought home after battle. At night I sit reading just above him on the classical balcony. The mansion contracts and creaks after the day's baking sun, and as does my ancient Bottengoms Farm in the Stour Valley, pegged together much the same moment as when Raleigh was settling Roanoke. 'Many writers have come here – to write!' There is certainly something professional about the great house, something serious. 'William Faulkner worked here – often. And

Thornton Wilder, a friend of father's.' The library is a dream, with more white pillars and proper mahogany library-steps for reaching the top shelves, and long runs of novels, plays and poetry. There are rare histories of the Carolinas and eclectic volumes of Anglican theology including, praise be, Evelyn Underhill's *Mysticism,* the very thing I need for the playlet. I find Faulkner's *The Reivers,* published in 1962, the year of his death. It is about a boy who 'borrows' his grandfather's chauffeur and automobile in 1905 Jefferson, for a trip to Memphis. It is written entirely in sweet dialogue – the kind which runs away with a novelist, and is perhaps Faulkner's running away from this life. A clickerty fan twizzled from the high ceiling and I feel that Mizz Charlotte will soon enter. I browse for hours and then return to their order a small mountain of books. I start the playlet. Dame Julian and Miss Underhill are at tea at Pleshey with some six centuries between them, not that it matters. One is wise, one is scholarly.

Evelyn: Isn't it amazing? I can reach out and touch you! I can see you and understand you!

How easy plays are to write. I leave my characters to cover the ground between *c* 1400 and *c* 1925 and go off to explore my mansion. Before leaving it to me, my immeasurably thoughtful hostess introduced me to Caswell County. Often it is only by showing a visitor our own sights that we ourselves begin to see what they are. We passed through townlets with spacious empty stores and through Milton where Thomas Day, the magnificent cabinet-maker created fine furniture for the antebellum drawing rooms. Day had arrived in 1823, from where nobody knows, and denying that he was a negro. He married a black woman and employed slaves. It was all very difficult. It was for Mrs Day's sake that the inhabitants of Milton persuaded the North

Carolinian General Assembly to amend the 1827 act forbidding migrant 'free Negroes' to enter the state. Thomas Day was their Chippendale and Milton suspended its racism for his mantels, stairs, beds and chairs. What a bargain Caswell County struck, not for humanity but for pragmatism. We drove through lovely aromatic forests.

Woods there were in abundance, noted the first Europeans to see them. 'Fair fields and plains . . . good and wholesome air . . . sweet and odiferous flowers . . . trees greater and better than any in Europe,' raved Verrazano, as he rounded Cape Fear in 1524. But even paradise has to be managed. Heaven has to be dug, felled, trimmed, shaped, labour not at all suitable for those chosen by God to dwell therein. And so the enslaved Africans were shipped in. The Confederate lad under the front lawn gave his life to keep them arriving. As we journeyed, I found myself thinking of John White returning to Devon with his paintings of milkweed, cardinals, plantains, Algonquin Indians, fireflies and woodpeckers – 'Maraseequo: a woodpecker of this bigness,: meaning the red-headed woodpecker, of course. Governor White, with his portraits of waders, fishes, but not one of Sir Walter's settlers, who were never seen or heard of again. Their site has become the most tenderly archaeologised few acres in the United States, its greatest yield an English sickle. Was there time to sow and reap America's primal cornfield?

Caswell County is notorious Klan country. Back home we still manage to gloss over our part in the 'West India Trade,' kidding ourselves that it was more sugar than slaves. In Caswell County the evidence of buying and selling people remains all over the place, and remains, too, so normal as not to prick the conscience. The black woman who comes each day to cook my dinner asks a lot of questions. 'Tell me, who is your First Lady, the Queen Elizabeth or the Mrs Thatcher?' She has not been out of North Carolina but her son, who is a soldier, is married to a German girl. 'We are Baptists. Come to our church on Sunday if you are a Christian.' Baptist churches with sharp white spires are all over the countryside, and too small for everyone to get inside, so they rise above huge outdoor congregations. The cook and I have many conversations. She laughs a lot, often shaking her head at the absurdity of things. Does it hurt her, the big bell in the yard which called the slaves in from over the fields, over a hundred of them on this plantation? Does it hurt her, the shopping-list of black men and women in the library? Some of their descendants bear my hostess's name. Some lounge around the courthouse in Yanceyville. Caswell County is Alex Haley's county, a place where everyone's roots still show, where they still lie raw above ground.

We all intended to meet Reynolds Price before we flew home but, alas, he is very ill. Price is among the latest and best of North Carolina's writers. Though not far from Duke University, we may not call. Price's epicentre is Macon, a small town four counties to the east and situated on the Virginia border. It inspired his autobiographical fiction, *The Names and Faces of Heroes* and *A Long and Happy Life*. Stephen Spender knows him of course. Visiting writers call on native writers in the States in the nineteenth century tradition, and Stephen is the doyen of visiting writers. Back at Tara, as I am beginning to call my lordly house, I am visited by my neighbour, the artist Maud Gatewood, a bluff, kind woman who paints not unlike David Hockney, only girls. Maud takes me to the Dan River and then across the bridge to Virginia, then to see her mother, then to see her house. Her tall girls crowd the studio. 'I studied *under Oscar Kokoschka*' though where does he come in? Like Harry and Eva's house it hides from the sun. A beautiful carved and painted horse from a roundabout takes pride of place in the cool interior and makes a nice ornament. Maud salts glasses for tequila and jollies the talk along. It is enormously pleasurable to be with her. Iridescent humming-birds sip honeyed water from little vials on the window-sills, their wing motion so rapid that the green of their bodies becomes no more than a stain of air. Heart-pine and shrubs press against the clapboarding. Whilst the old Caswell houses began their existence in broad clearings, the new ones go up in deep shade.

On the last night I sit reading as usual above the soldier's grave. A thunderstorm blows up and there are crashings from the park. Turmoil. I thought of the son of the house hurrying up here to the balcony to watch the lightening and the slaves cowering in the cabins, and sparks being struck from their bell. There are hundreds more soldiers like him down the road at Raleigh in a cemetery described at the time they were buried as 'a suitable and permanent resting place for the heroes of crushed hopes.' Raleigh had surrendered to General Sherman just the day before Lincoln's murder. The house was sparkling new then. Sherman's army poured past it and all through the Carolinas, wrecking their economy and thus preventing such glorious architecture from being updated or replaced, and causing the slaves to be emancipated but only to suffer a different degradation for the next one hundred years.

'Death,' wrote Raleigh, 'Thou hast drawn together all the far'stretched greatness, all the pride, cruelty and ambition of man and covered it all over with these two narrow words, *Hic jacet!*'